The Imagery of the

Frits H Julius

The Imagery of
the Zodiac

Floris Books

Translated by Tony Langham and Plym Peters

First published in Dutch under the title
De Beeldentaal van de Dierenriem by Uitgeverij Vrij Geestesleven, Zeist
First published in English in 1994 by Floris Books
Reprinted 2008

British Library CIP Data available

ISBN 978-086315-177-4

Printed in Great Britain by Cpod

Contents

Foreword

Nowadays it is more of a challenge than ever to publish anything about the signs of the zodiac, because the author's intentions are easily misinterpreted. This book entirely avoids the search for a specific link between a constellation and a particular person, and the reader will find very little about astrological traditions and goals. There is only one area where astrological tradition is referred to, and that is in the naming and order of the signs of the zodiac.

We are involved here with a subject which makes the highest demands on our skills to penetrate the connection between the constellations and the life of individuals. The author believes that it is possible to gain completely clear and certain insights in this field only if our consciousness is raised to a level which can be achieved solely by rigorous inner training. In general, astrologers do not practise at this level. Among them there are undoubtedly serious seekers, who have at their disposal an important store of traditional knowledge, methods and numerous experiences. There is no reason to doubt the possibility of obtaining important indications regarding our destiny by drawing up horoscopes. However, this does not necessarily mean that their work is of a scientific nature.

Astrology pursued at the superficial and speculative level which is only too common, can be avoided by following a more rigorous path. The first requirement on this path of serious study and exercise is to stop looking only in one's own mirror. We should not rest until we have learnt to see not just our own self, but beyond to a wider community of people, and finally to an all-encompassing universe. We can only truly understand our own self when we can derive our characteristic qualities from this whole. When we have made this effort, the signs of the zodiac may acquire something approaching a human quality. It is possible to learn to use them as though they are a large picture book. Leafing through this book, one finds a wonderful series of images, which reflect the parallels and connections between the natural world order and human existence. In this work we will use this picture book primarily as a textbook on psychology, or even as a companion to understanding social behaviour.

The lengthy study on which this book was based was only possible with the help of the guidelines and methods which we owe to the spiritual science of Rudolf Steiner. However, the writer has endeavoured to use this body of knowledge in such a way that the reader unfamiliar with Steiner's work will be able to comprehend fully his line of thought.

1. The Signs of the Zodiac and Human Consciousness

The origins of the signs of the zodiac are rooted in the mythology of antiquity. Modern man* has developed a view of the world based on the conscious processing of perceptions. The world appears to the senses as an infinite multiplicity of individual details. We meet this multiplicity with concepts and use these to weave them together as far as possible to form a whole. Whenever we succeed in fitting a detail in its proper place in our conceptual world, we feel that we have taken another step on the road to truth.

In the days when mythology was a living force, the figures of the gods and other spiritual beings immediately appeared in man's consciousness as images. At that time there was no question of ordinary people having to struggle laboriously for the truth. Generally speaking, everything that was necessary for the gratification of spiritual needs entered the mind directly. These images actually contained an element of divine forces. There was not yet a gap between man's inner being and the content of the world. But at that time man could only think, feel and will very little himself. It was the gods who felt in him, thought in him and willed in him. The old stories about gods intervening in the affairs of man reflect a profound reality. Humankind as a whole was at a stage which is now found only in children. Humankind was safeguarded, cared for and led with the greatest concern by higher beings. In another respect, humankind was also at a more childlike stage of development. The development of our constitution had also progressed less far than it has now. The forces that led us

---

* For this and subsequent uses of the word 'man' the author is using the term inclusively to refer to both man and woman.

were at the same time the creators of our organization. Thus the characteristic feature of the mythological developmental stage of man can be described as follows: in mythological consciousness man interpreted the forces that comprise both the world and his own organization as living images. At the time when this applied, virtually the whole of life was a matter of religious cults.

The capacity for abstract thought without imagery developed very slowly. The effect of divine forces directly penetrated our thinking less and less, while increasingly attention was focused on the world of the senses. Nowadays our thinking is so desolate that it is virtually stimulated only by the riddles produced by the senses. This thinking produced by the senses is derived from the highest creative forces, but they no longer have a direct effect, so that they cannot influence us directly either. As a result, we now have an open field in which we can train our independent strength ourselves. Undisturbed by the strength of the powers which created us and our world, we are free to think for ourselves and to draw the consequences of our own thoughts in our actions, whether these are right or wrong, constructive or destructive. Thus we are in the process of acquiring a powerful force: self-awareness. We are beings with a source within ourselves. We are on the way to becoming beings who think and act entirely from ourselves, free beings. We are called upon to become kings of creation.

However, there is a high price to pay for this tremendous conquest in the form of a great decline of divine forces. We have become lonely, and not only lonely but also poorer, for the loss of imagery from our thinking represents a terrible impoverishment of our consciousness.

Therefore it is not surprising that in some people this condition has produced a profound longing, though the strength of this longing is often not recognized. For them, the totality of man's spiritual endeavours amounts to a great struggle to achieve a new link with the depths of the world. By contrast, other people have accepted the present condition and their acts correspond to their lost and confused thoughts. The result is that the forces which they set into motion clash chaotically. These are the people who have long been leading society along a path of conflict and destruction in an arbitrary fashion.

When history is viewed in this light, it is clear that there is only one way out of the valley of horrors which we inhabit at the moment. We must consciously and freely unite with the forces which put creation into our hands.

For our inner selves, this means that we must find a transition to a new consciousness of imagery. The instinctive pictorial consciousness was replaced by self-conscious thinking. If we are to retain what we have conquered and then transcend this, we will have to develop a self-aware pictorial consciousness. In the past, divine forces worked inside man despite him, and evoked images in him. This was the language in which these forces spoke to man. Now we will have to begin by forming these images ourselves, and, bearing the images in the form of a question, go forward to meet the divine forces. This means that the forces will be able to speak to us again because the images are an area to which they have access. We will have to start by forming these images in the hope that they will be given life.

In this book we have taken the traditional signs of the zodiac from antiquity, and given them new life with the help of perceptions provided by nature. We could also say that we are concentrating on the imprint left by the effect of divine forces on nature, using the traditional signs of the zodiac. In this way we hope to bring life into abstract thinking, and fill it with universal concepts. In the following chapters we will alternate between a thinking based on observation and imagery and one that is rooted in abstract explanation.

Meanwhile, we are already living in a world which is chaotic as a consequence of false ways of thinking. In this day and age, inner activity alone, which is restricted to philosophy, has less weight than ever before. The question is not only how we can once again restore harmony between our inner life and the cosmos. We will have to fight a tremendous battle, a gentle battle, a healing battle against the force of chaos. We should not rest until our thoughts are permeated with new life to such an extent that they give us the strength to ensure that the cosmic order has a fertile and creative effect on society.

2. The Difference between Humans and Animals

Most of the names of the signs of the zodiac refer to animals, and therefore we would like to discuss these with reference to the central laws on which the animal kingdom is based.

Although there is such a diversity among animals that one might be inclined to classify them in different categories of nature, they do have one thing in common: all their experiences and activities are accompanied by perceptions, that is, varying degrees of consciousness. All animals are ensouled creatures.

It is as though there is a natural force which has the power to create animals freely, while raising the following problem: 'How can I create ensouled creatures which are linked with every conceivable area of nature in the most profound sense?' Or to put it the other way round: 'How can I give birth to an ensouled creature based on every conceivable area of nature?' When you remember that animal life exists from the poles to the bottom of the deepest seas, and that there are animals who live only on dry wood, or others on the horns of dead antelopes, it is clear that this problem has been thoroughly explored, and that the results of this endeavour have certainly been successful.

There are only a few situations of which some animal has not been able to make use. However, every species is adapted to its own more or less restricted situation, to the exclusion of all other possibilities. It is and remains an answer which only corresponds to one particular question.

This is one of the great contrasts with man, who can constantly pose new questions and participate in new situations. In this way man develops scientifically and, with the help of technology, succeeds in inhabiting or at least visiting every possible area of the world. However, man is also fully aware of the problems he has set himself. He is a self-conscious being. An animal cannot set itself any questions. The animal is an answer to a problem which has been posed; it is an answer to a problem of which it is not aware, and answers it by dreaming and acting. One could almost say that it *lives* the answer. It is completely bound up in the solution to the problem, while man confronts the problem. Thus man is not only a ensouled creature, he is a consciously spiritual creature. The wisdom which governs the whole connection with the environment remains unconscious and in the background in the animal world, but is consciously present in man in every individual.

Perhaps the best way to demonstrate this difference is in the techniques used by man and animal. A songbird which has reached a particular level of development can simply build a nest. It looks for suitable material and constructs something which is exactly right for its own body, eggs, and its young, as well as being perfectly insulated and often very well camouflaged. All the other members of its species make virtually the same nest. Man has to learn all sorts of things from outside; there is very little he can do from within. When he has learnt the right things, he is able to make discoveries, that is, he can extend and renew his skills independently. If he wishes to build a dwelling, which could be compared to a bird's nest, he would first have to practise at great length, and even then would probably make some terrible mistakes. But with the help of technology, man can learn to do everything animals can, and much more. Our boats swim faster than fish, our cars run faster than horses, and our airplanes fly faster and higher than birds.

In animals the area on which creation is based remains in the background, despite all their skills. In man the capacity for creation surfaces individually. In this context we can discover that animals have a great but completely unconscious wisdom in all their activities and experiences. Man's wisdom is of a *self-acquiring* and *creative* nature.

It is characteristic of animals that they are completely bound to a particular environment. To a significant extent, every animal lives in a one-sided world without freedom. One could even say that the more one-sided the animal is with regard to the area it inhabits, the more it is a typical animal. Examples that spring to mind are the wonderful fluttering of butterflies in the free light and air of the atmosphere, and the way in which fish move through water with their flowing movements. In contrast, it is a human characteristic to transcend these restrictions and overcome such one-sided aspects. Of course, certain professions require specialization, concentrating on a particular area with one-sided skills. For the time being, this is essential. But it also gives rise to the great problem which is inherent in many modern professions: how can I develop as a human being, despite my work? People are more human in a real sense as they transcend their environment and become less one-sided — one could say, as they acquire more characteristics. Of course, they also have to control the environment, but rather than this referring to one particular area of the environment, it refers to all areas.

When we realize this, we are ready to learn from the fundamental wisdom of the animal world which is reflected in the signs of the zodiac.

In order to understand the essence of a particular animal, as well as the task that it has in nature as a whole, it is necessary to observe not only its structure and characteristics, but above all the way in which it fits into its environment. The most profound quality of its animal character can be found in the animal's interrelationship with its environment. We begin to consider the instincts, an area in which there is great wisdom far exceeding ordinary human understanding. This brings us to a simple guideline for our study: we concentrate first on those organs which the animal uses to maintain its link with the environment, that is, the sensory organs, the mouth, the legs, horns or wings.

Such an approach is rarely found in contemporary scientific literature, but it can be found in Goethe's zoological studies, and in some cases these ideas were fully elaborated. Goethe summarized many of them in his poem 'Die Metamorphose der Tiere.' Here he formulated his rule that every animal forms a harmonious whole in which all the separate components interact with great wisdom. But it is as though there is a force present in every species which attempts to break down this harmony and to propel the organization towards a particular one-sidedness. Certain organs are developed to an exaggerated extent again and again, while others are proportionately neglected. A cow has a bone in its forehead which has grown to form horns, but it has lost its upper incisors. The lion has tremendous teeth and claws, but nothing which approaches horns. Goethe called this rule the key to understanding all forms. He also strongly emphasizes the link between the animal's structure and the environment, and vice versa.

Looking at these ideas in relation to the study of the creatures of the zodiac, we can see that each creature possesses a characteristic skill in which it excels over the others, as well as a corresponding shortcoming in which it is inferior to the others. All the signs have extreme characteristics and widely differing attitudes to the surrounding world. Each possesses a high degree of the one-sided nature which Goethe refers to in his poem. The surprising thing is that the relationships between these one-sided aspects are governed by strict rules. In our discussions we will devote special attention to the most striking interconnections, particularly to those between the signs which are opposite each other. These always have a polar relation, that is, they belong together and form a contrast to the opposite sign in every respect. A pronounced ability on one

---

*   A full development of these ideas can be found in *Man and Animal* by
    Hermann Poppelbaum (Anthroposophical Publishing Co, London 1960).

side appears as a disability on the other, while the strength on the second side is a weakness on the first side.

This forms a significant extension of the law described by Goethe in his treatises on comparative anatomy, and in his poem. In these he refers to a separate rule for every individual animal; this rule also gives rise to an interconnection and interaction between completely different creatures. These connections can also be found in creatures other than the signs of the zodiac. We have arrived at one of the fundamental truths of the world structure.

We cannot go much further in this direction with regard to nature. However, this discovery has greater significance because it is a key to a greater understanding of people, and in this way it can open the door to the greatest possible innovations in our society. This aspect will be elaborated in a later chapter.

3. The Constellations in the Seasons

A brief outline of the movement of the sun

In the course of this chapter we will look at the signs of the zodiac in relation to the movement of the sun around the earth and through the seasons.

We will begin by briefly describing this movement as it is perceived by the observer on earth, our starting point being what is usually known as the 'apparent' movement. For the moment we will ignore all sorts of explanations of the so-called true course of the movements of the sun and earth, as well as the fact that the position and the movement of the sun can be completely different, and even opposite at different places on the earth.

The most striking *movement of the sun* is its *daily* movement. Every day the sun rises above the earth on the eastern horizon, then it arcs above the southern horizon to the west, and finally disappears below the earth. In summer the arc begins and ends further to the north, though it still rises high in the sky. In winter the arc begins and ends further to the south, and only rises a little way above the horizon.

It is far more difficult to follow the *annual movement of the sun* in relation to the stars. If we were able to see the stars during the day, we would see that the sun moves very slowly in the opposite direction to its daily motion. In relation to the stars it always moves from west to east. The movement of the moon, which is easy to observe, is very similar, but is twelve times as fast. The time taken for the sun to complete one revolution, returning to the same position, is called a year.

It is particularly significant that, in its annual movement, the sun moves towards the northern skies between January and June, during winter and spring, and therefore increasingly takes up a higher position, while it moves closer to the southern skies during summer and autumn, between July and December, so that it increasingly takes up a lower position. The seasons are closely connected with this movement, and the annual orbit of the sun is a large circle in the heavens which traverses the signs of the zodiac.

There are twelve signs of the zodiac. The names appear in the order in which the sun moves through them. In addition, the signs which are opposite each other in the sky are also placed opposite each other here. This is particularly significant in connection with the contrasts between these signs.

Capricorn	*Cancer*
Aquarius	*Leo*
Pisces	*Virgo*
Aries	*Libra*
Taurus	*Scorpio*
Gemini	*Sagittarius*

A careful study of the movement of the sun in relation to the constellation reveals that the sun reaches its zenith as it moves through Gemini, and its lowest point as it moves through Sagittarius. These points are very slowly shifting, and two thousand years ago, the highest point was in Cancer, and the lowest in Capricorn. Because of this we still say that the sun reaches its highest point in the *sign* of Cancer and its lowest point in the *sign* of Capricorn.

Thus we must make a distinction between the *constellations* and the *signs* of the zodiac. The constellations of the zodiac are the groups of stars which can actually be seen in the sky. The signs of the zodiac are names which are given to particular points in the annual course of the sun, based in the constellations in which these points were located two thousand years ago.

The constellations and the signs are gradually moving further apart. While two thousand years ago they co-incided, today the sign of Cancer is in the constellation of Gemini, and the sign of Capricorn is in the constellation of Sagittarius. Our whole study is concerned primarily with the movement of the sun, and thus it is related to the signs of the zodiac and not to the constellations. This is not arbitrary, but as we will shortly see, in the sign of Cancer the movement of the sun is related to the essence of the crab, etc.

Perhaps this could be explained as follows. The events which occur on and around the earth are reflections of the laws of the zodiac. Such events as the seasonal changes of the year, which take place according to an established order, represent a very special cosmic constellation as it appeared two thousand years ago.

By way of clarification, a few diagrams are given below to show the movement of the sun.

If we look only at the highest position of the sun every day at about midday, and its lowest position every night at about midnight, it is fairly easy to form an idea of the change in its position in relation to the horizon during the course of the year (see Figure 1).

If the daily movement of the sun is also studied, it is clear that at its highest position the sun describes by far the larger part of its path above the horizon, and the smaller part below. At the lowest position, this is the other way round. When day and night are equal in the spring and autumn, the equinox, the two parts of the path are the same size. This is represented in Figure 2 and can be summarized as follows:

Winter: Sun mainly below earth	Movement upwards accelerates.
Spring: Sun mainly above earth	Movement upwards slows down.
Summer: Sun mainly above earth	Movement downwards accelerates.
Autumn: Sun mainly below earth	Movement downwards slows down.

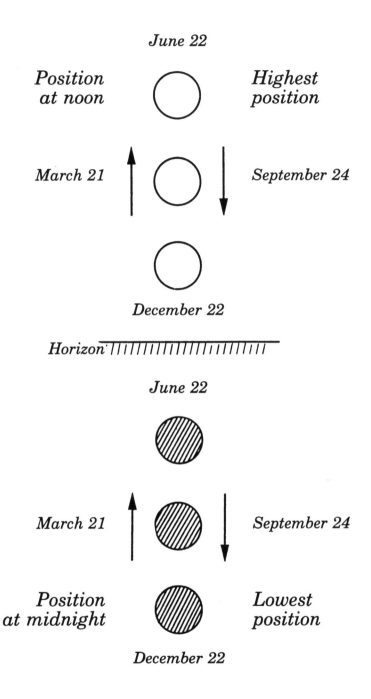

Figure 1.

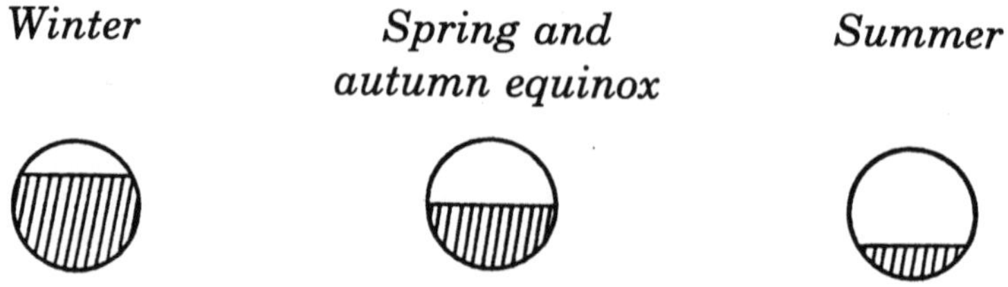

Winter	*Spring and autumn equinox*	*Summer*

Figure 2.

Around the summer and winter solstice there is little perceptible vertical movement, while around the spring and autumn equinox the upward and downward movements are fastest. Thus the whole character of this movement is similar to that of a pendulum.

We can summarize the sun's movement through the zodiac during the course of the year in Figure 3.

Lightness and weight

The movement of the sun through the seasons is a cosmic drama. If we use only pure mathematics or the usual scientific concepts, it is impossible to decipher the imagery which relates to the seasons of the year. There is a tremendous amount of wisdom in the relationships in nature which cannot be grasped if we use only those concepts. But if we wish to unlock the secrets of the structure of the cosmos, we need new keys, as we have lost the old ones.

One of the first keys is the insight that the whole of nature is governed by the polarity between lightness and weight. This idea is one of the first that Rudolf Steiner developed in his scientific lectures.*

As inhabitants of the earth's surface, the realm of weight is below us, while that of lightness is around and above us. Below us everything is closed, rigid and impenetrable. Above, everything becomes increasingly ethereal, radiant

* *Light. First Scientific Lecture-Course* (Steiner Schools Fellowship, Forest Row 1987).

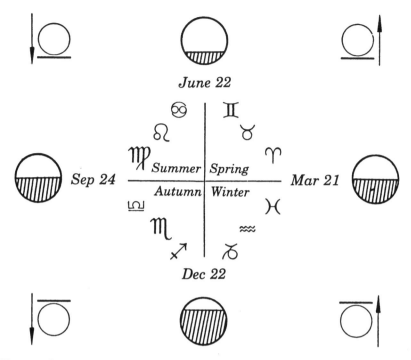

Figure 3.

and active. In the realm of weight there is total darkness; the greatest force attracting to the centre of the earth. On the other hand, light shines down on us from all around.

These matters are easier to understand if we look at the role they play for living creatures. For example, a creature such as the eagle is adapted to the area of lightness by its whole nature and structure. It is true that its body consists partly of hard, dead matter, but when flying or gliding, this matter becomes part of such a radiant interplay of form and movement oriented towards the periphery of the earth, that the bird is able to lift itself away from the earth, through the forces of lightness. Concentrating on the ultimate organ of light, the eye, it is clear that the eagle's sharp gaze can see further and more accurately than that of most other creatures.

On the other hand, a creature such as the cow is unremittingly adapted towards heaviness by the very structure of its body and its behaviour.

Man is different. In his build and posture, he achieves a perfect balance between heaviness and lightness. He is called upon to allow each tendency to come into its own, though nowadays we can discern a predominance towards heaviness.

One of the great founders of modern science, Galileo, discovered the law of gravity and the law of the pendulum, increasing our understanding of weight and matter. Since his time, science has increasingly followed this path — even the study of light was described in terms of rays of particles and waves. Thus an attempt was made to explain the phenomena of light using concepts developed for describing weight. Of course, it was not possible to deal in this way with the higher sensory qualities such as sound, colour, smell and taste. The problem posed by these sensory experiences was solved by explaining them away as illusions. Events of a more mechanical nature supposedly affected us, triggering the illusion of these qualities. The qualities thus do not correspond with any outside reality. This modern materialistic scientific approach does not really give us a basis for an understanding of the human soul and its experiences. For when man seeks to establish a conscious relationship with his environment, the sensory qualities undeniably play a major role.

However, it is possible to arrive at a completely different understanding of the world of the higher senses. Goethe led the way with his study of colour. The concepts he introduced for the phenomena of light and colour were directly developed from the way in which he perceived them. Thus he succeeded in penetrating the qualities of colour so profoundly that he was able to produce a detailed explanation of the specific effect of colour on the soul. In this way he laid the foundation for a science which is fertile soil for the human soul, allowing for a completely new relationship between man and the world.

Goethe's achievements contribute a very special basis for our work. He not only taught us to take the qualities of light and colour seriously and to understand them, but he offered us an approach to the phenomenon of colour which allows us to penetrate other areas. Following this approach leads on to unexpected ideas and to a completely new and more profound relationship with reality.

To grasp this approach let us use a comparison. Anyone following Goethe's example approaches nature like a drama on stage. One must concentrate entirely on what is shown in order to understand the intentions the author and director wish to express.

If colour and sound are considered to be illusions, and reality is sought in the vibrations accompanying them; if the qualities of perceptions are not taken seriously, and discussions concentrate on molecules and atoms, it is like members of the audience who are only interested in the mechanics and effects behind the scenes and in the director's technical skill while the whole meaning of the·play is lost to them. Although science and technology have developed to a high degree as a result of this approach, it should not be forgotten that there would be no mechanics and theatrical effects if there were no play to perform.

Modern science concentrates virtually exclusively on the side of nature which could be called the technical aspect, and undervalues those phenomena in which the sense of nature is most strongly expressed.

In addition to this, there is another reason why it would be constructive to observe cosmic phenomena as the performance of a great drama. When we identify the main *dramatis personae,* the sun and the earth, and characterize them, it is immediately obvious that these could be considered as the archetypal example of all dramas. One could not conceive of a more irreconcilable contrast than that between these two protagonists, and yet they are in constant interaction with moments of tension and relaxation, joy and tragedy.

The sun is completely dominated by light; it is radiance and light itself by definition, illuminating the colours around us, stimulating life and activity all around. In contrast, the earth is on the side of weight; it brings dull darkness, which extinguishes the glow of colours, brings inertia and rigidifies everything it touches.

Throughout the spring the light, celestial sun frees itself from the earth and rises higher day by day until it attains a height from which it can fully unfold its radiant nature. In the autumn the bringer of light sinks lower and lower into an area that is alien to it and in a sense, even hostile, and we see its radiance and creative force increasingly restricted.

However, this describes only the two main movements. If we follow the relationship between the sun and the earth in detail, we see that the nature of this relationship is constantly changing. Every movement and position can be read as a dramatic sign which expresses a particular mood, even a particular character or conflict. We shall see that in observing this we are approaching a level of truth closely related to the secrets of the signs of the zodiac.

These insights can bear fruit only if we learn to use them to overcome certain inhibitions inherent in our present ways of thinking. In order to enter fully into our own experience of the phenomena, we must forget both our concepts of the movements of the sun and earth, as well as the knowledge that while for us the sun sinks lower and lower, it rises in the opposite hemisphere.

A moment's reflection immediately reveals that the natural processes which take place in the weather and in the life processes of plants, animals and man, are directly related to the relationship of the sun to our own position. The way in which the sun is perceived from other parts of the earth, or indeed from other parts of the universe, is of no importance in this respect. Thus, in a sense, we are using a geocentric starting point in the most basic way, and we will examine the ideas this perspective produces. In this way we hope to shed some light on the cosmic order, in so far as this is related to life-processes on earth. For this approach the heliocentric worldview, which is perfectly valid as such, is entirely beside the point.

Ascending and descending signs

To learn how to read the imagery of the zodiac more effectively we shall survey the creatures of the signs through which the sun passes when it rises, as well as those through which it passes when descending.

The ascending signs include three animals — the goat (Capricorn), the ram (Aries), and the bull (Taurus) — which have horns. The descending signs include two animals with pincers — the crab (Cancer), and the scorpion (Scorpio) — and two with claws — the lion (Leo) and the eagle. Horns are used to repel other creatures and therefore mainly serve to widen the distance between two creatures. Claws and pincers are used for bringing other animals or objects closer, serving to reduce their proximity. This shows how precisely the imagery expresses cosmic events. In the ascending movement of the sun the distance between the sun and the earth actually becomes greater every day, while it gets smaller as the sun moves down. Later on, we will see that the other creatures of the ascending signs, Aquarius, Pisces and Gemini, all have an aspect of flowing out or radiance, while the other creatures of the descending signs, the scales (Libra), the virgin (Virgo), and the archer (Sagittarius), represent a surrender to earthly forces, a drawing together or even an approach. One of the things expressed by the signs is the alternating proximity of the sun and the earth.

It is also striking to note that the descending signs are all creatures with a more or less developed nurturing nature, such as a character like Virgo, who is completely prepared for taking in and looking after a child, or a character such as Sagittarius, who also has a special relationship with children. The ascending signs are only animals with few nurturing qualities. Fish are even quite careless about their offspring. These facts are easier to understand when they are read as symbols, just as the use of horns and claws are symbols. Reproduction in itself always signifies a separation. In contrast, nurturing is based on the tendency to hold together something that has to go its own way in the end. Thus once again, this separation is found in the upward movement of the sun and the coming together in the downward movement. This completely corresponds with the above.

The succession of signs as a dramatic image of the sun's path

What we have learned so far can now be used to represent a cycle of the year in terms of imagery.

Throughout the spring the sun climbs up from the depths in accordance with its character of light. Then, when it begins to sink down again to the depths after the solstice, it becomes a *crab* withdrawing from the wide open space of its surroundings in a scuttling backward movement leading into a narrow cranny.

But still its power is not spent. Now it turns into a *lion*, and grasps deep into the living body of the earth with all the strength of its fiery force of light. The nature of the earth becomes the *virgin* with the sun-child in her lap. The wild and mighty strength becomes tranquil; the atmosphere is completely pure and transparent, although it often attempts to shroud everything in fine veils of mist. The sun sinks faster than ever, and, at the equinox when the day and night are equally long, the balance of the world's scales, on which the sun is resting, tips down to the depths. But already the sun strives for equilibrium: the movement is held in check and gradually slows down.

Despite this, and despite the fact that the hope of new light and life is not lost, something terrible has to happen. The once so radiant sun is increasingly bound to the earth and robbed of all its life-giving strength. It is still the bringer of light, it can still make the odd little plant grow, but when we realize what it has lost, we also become aware of the power of the forces of death surrounding it. It crawls into the depths like a *scorpion* and is embraced by the kingdom of death. Compared to its former glory, it has become a dried-up, desiccated thing, just as the scorpion is a miserable, fearsome creature.

And still the sun sinks even further into the veil of darkness. Yet it is as though there is a tremendous tension resisting it. It sinks down deeper and deeper, though more and more slowly and the tension becomes greater and greater as it increasingly resists being bound to the underworld. Now it is a *centaur*, a higher creature bound to a lower, fully experiencing this tragedy and violently rejecting being bound.

Finally, when the full threat of a drop into the limitless abyss of the depths of the world has passed, it starts to rise again, and it is like the *goat*. Its whole being is in conflict with the earth forces pulling it down. In a violent conflict with the environment it regains its own essence and with indomitable strength it seeks its own place in the heights.

However, the signs of the zodiac do not all refer to tension and conflict. In *Aquarius*, the noble figure of a man with an overflowing water container, we recognize a lofty peace. Among all the creatures of the earth, only man is a creature who can gain the greatest healing power from the deepest tragedy. The sun in the bleakness of winter contains something which is above all a gift of man: in the middle of the cold darkness it begins to draw new life out of the earth, just as man can gain the highest blessing from deepest sorrow.

With ever-increasing strength the sun now awakens the forces of life. It is still largely bound to the dark depths, but every day it rises higher and enters further into the kingdom of light. It is during this time that it rises fastest. It is as though it is building up momentum for the mighty arc of light which it establishes above the kingdom of darkness in summer. It is like Pisces, the *fish*, which still really belongs below the surface, but constantly rises above the surface in a shining curve. Just as the fish belongs in water, the life-giving element, all the buds and seeds are filled with an inner radiant life force, while outwardly they are only just beginning to open, their new forms appearing in the kingdom of light.

When day and night are the same length, the sun's character of light has already conquered the depths, and it rises higher and higher with an irresistible force. Daily it drives back the darkness. Like Aries, the *ram*, which pushes aside its opponent with strong thrusts of its horns, and wins victory with its own will, the sun's character of light comes into its own without mercy. The whole of nature joins in; everywhere we find the kingdom of light unfolding and a great breakthrough is made through the rigid bonds.

Then it rises further still, though more slowly. Its light is not yet accompanied by the killing heat of the time of Leo, the *lion*, but is now achieving the zenith of its life-giving force. Life is never more productive, and growth is never so strong as at this time. Compared with its characteristics at other times of the year, the sun is now like Taurus, the *bull*, in the animal kingdom. More than others, this creature lives surrounded by blossoming, blooming life forces, completely taken over by the powerful digestion and fertile productivity.

Although it has already risen high, it still continues to rise. The full beauty of its ethereal character of light comes into its own. It sweeps over the surface of the earth in a magnificent arc, barely descending into the dark depths. It leaves behind everything that is dark and heavy, and even threatens to escape the heights. The surface of the earth has become a wonderful reflection of the sun, as at no other time of year. Nowhere else is there so much radiant colour, so many blossoming plants, so much singing of birds, such a wealth of flowers and butterflies. The whole of nature is an airy playfulness, as though the sun and the earth are two joyful children. This is the time of the Gemini, the *twins*, in which the great polarity between lightness and heaviness is represented in the contrast between the sun and the earth, just as the strongest inner tensions took place in the time of Aquarius. The sun and the earth now appear as *Gemini*.

Just as the great forces which cause the sun to change direction in the depths of winter could only be symbolized by the wild clambering of Capricorn, we can understand that in contrast only a creature as hardened and earthbound as a crab could represent the tremendous transition following the summer solstice. In the sign of *Cancer* the sun begins to abandon its own character of light, and allows itself to be bound by the constricting bonds of the depths.

We now have an overview of the succession of the constellations in the course of the year. Although the transitions in the movements of the sun are gradual, the succession of these images is quite dramatic. Certainly when the successive creatures represented by the signs of the zodiac are carefully observed, it is clear that they show rich and surprising diversity.

A detailed description of each sign of the zodiac and its relationship to its opposite follows in the next chapter.

4. The Living Images of the Signs of the Zodiac

We have seen how the signs of the zodiac reveal the curious fact that the nature of particular creatures characterize the movement of the sun and the interaction between the sun and the earth at any given time.

Now we will do the opposite, examining to what extent the nature of the creatures of the zodiac is an illustration of their corresponding sun-earth constellation. We will describe them in three groups of four creatures, each with its own character. We begin with the cross of Taurus, Leo, Scorpio and Aquarius.

Scorpio

Between October 24 and November 23 the sun's arc has already largely sunk below the earth, and yet it steadfastly continues into the depths. The light it emits is faint, and still it grows dimmer. It has virtually no life-giving strength left; in nature the last leaves fall from the trees. The buds have virtually stopped growing.

Scorpions are creatures which flee from the light. During the day they hide in dark crevices and holes. They can take us by surprise in a rather unpleasant way. In warmer climates it can happen that when you go to bed, you can suddenly be stung very painfully — the scorpion has found your bed to be a good hiding place. This is characteristic of the Scorpio character: quite unexpectedly, and without time to think of an honest defence, one can be violently attacked. Only when it is dark outside does a scorpion crawl out of its crevice, living a concealed life, even when it is darting about, hunting for food. It moves forward holding its two pincers in front of it, rather like a crab's pincers. Its long articulated tail, with the sting at the end, sometimes points backwards but is usually threateningly curved forwards over the head. A scorpion is constantly ready to seize and sting its prey. It is able to kill large insects and spiders without endangering itself. It takes hold of its victim with its pincers, lifts it off the ground and holds it in front of its head at a safe distance rendering it powerless with its sting, while it carefully probes around for a weak spot. Then after a few convulsions the prey is finished off. Slowly and methodically, the scorpion starts to eat it. A scorpion sting is extremely painful and can even be fatal to humans.

The scorpion is a creature of contradiction, just like the November sun. It seems to *live* with the sole aim of demonstrating the power of *death*. In general, water has a life-giving power but the scorpion has a fluid poison in it which is used as a fatal weapon.

We should also mention the well-known belief that scorpions commit suicide when they are placed within a ring of fire. There is a story about a man who had a scorpion in a bottle in the dark. When he went up to the scorpion with a bright light, it pointed its sting at its own body, and as he withdrew the light, the sting was also drawn back. When he went on and brought the light closer, the scorpion killed itself. This is the true problem of the scorpion: life, which kills itself for no other reason than the fear of light.

Once when I was travelling in Italy, a small scorpion fell onto my hand as I opened a door. I immediately noticed how the creature flattened itself, pressing its tail right down, its pincers stretched out and legs spread out to the sides. Obviously this is the perfect position for a creature which lives in narrow crevices. But it is also an expressive attitude, particularly when it is compared to the eagle and the cow, as we will see in detail below. The scorpion is low on the ground, a 'flat' creature.

The scorpion's nurturing qualities are impressive. The

mother is very careful with her young. For several weeks she keeps them on her back. Throughout this time she does not use her sting, and therefore does not eat. There is a very beautiful description of this behaviour and of other habits of the scorpion in Fabre's *Souvenirs Entomologiques*.

Taurus

Between April 21 and May 22 the sun is above the earth for most of the time, and yet it continues to ascend steadily. The strength of its light is already great, but continues to increase. It is at this time that it emits the greatest life-giving force. Plants burst with life.

Cattle are large, strongly built creatures with a very rounded form. They are certainly not suited to hiding themselves or creeping around like a scorpion. The wild herds that live in the open on wide prairies do make sure that they stay well away from their enemies. They live surrounded by a wealth of brimming life, whether they enjoy the juicy grass which shoots up from the ground, or live off the young foliage of trees and bushes. It is only in the difficult seasons when it is very cold or dry that they occasionally have to fight to survive.

The build and life cycle of cattle indicates that their life element lies in the kingdom of solid earth forces. In many cows this can be seen in their shape: heavy, stiff legs, the ponderous build and the simple geometry of their form. The line of the back is often as straight as the horizon. The cow lets its head hang down to the earth, and even when standing it never fully raises it. Seen from the side, its body is almost a rectangle, and from behind, it is a well-filled circle — in short, a barrel.

In some breeds, such as the bison, the head hangs right down. This species is characterized even more than others by an unusually poorly developed eye.

It is quite awe-inspiring to see how cattle devote themselves to the task of filling themselves with vast quantities of food, and then thoroughly transforming it with their digestive organs.

Cattle graze patiently in broad lines, moving forward step by step. The head moves slowly from left to right and back again. The tongue is twisted round clumps of grass which are carefully torn away so that very few blades escape. It takes a long time for the cow to eat its fill. Then it lies down heavily with its dreamy head slightly raised. A bolus of food slides up through the throat and the cow starts to chew the cud. The lower jaw moves backwards and forwards at least sixty times, then it stops for a moment. The chewed cud moves down and more food comes up. What happens next inside the cow is every bit as thorough. Can there be another animal that digests its food as thoroughly as this creature? Certainly it shows the greatest thoroughness of all the creatures of the zodiac.

It is hardly surprising that this creature is of the utmost importance to others. A large part of human society has developed with the help of the great strength of cattle, and these creatures have enabled humankind to have a stronger connection with the earth. Without manure, the earth could not have borne enough life to support the human population, and if cattle had not been so good at transforming raw grass — too rough for our consumption — into milk and meat, it would not have been possible for such rich and sophisticated cultures. Our cows use their strength not only for themselves, but also to serve others. They constantly sacrifice themselves for the benefit of humankind and the world.

The bull has an even denser build than the cow: it is a mass of muscle. Usually it is calm, but at the same time you can see that it is always under great tension. It becomes a terrible creature when this tension is released in the form of rage. It lashes wildly with its tail, paws at the ground with its hooves, turning and swinging its head, and digs deep grooves in the earth with its horns. Suddenly it charges at its enemy with its full weight. If it charges at another bull, they fight with their heads locked together, eyes protruding, tongues lolling down. It takes smaller opponents on its horns with its head down, and then tosses them away in a powerful arch.

It is revealing to compare a creature, such as a bull fighting with its horns, with a predator fighting with claws. The bull fights with centrifugal force, tossing, stamping or flinging away everything around it. In contrast the lion engulfs its prey, sinking its teeth and claws into it with a centripetal movement. In the previous chapter we saw how this relates to the movement of the sun (see page 27).

Thus we have found differences between the behaviour of the cow and the bull, but nevertheless, they correspond in many respects. They incorporate the strongest earth forces in their build, and seek the greatest resistances. Whether these are through metabolic processes or wild feats of strength, their organization is always in balance, without restraint.

Taurus and Scorpio

Using Goethe's approach referred to in the Introduction, it is possible to contrast the scorpion and the bull in some detail. On one hand this relates to the seasons of the year, and on the other it is a key to human psychology.

There is no creature of the zodiac that is as strongly tied to the digestive processes as Taurus. It is completely at home in the weight of matter. But with its strong life force, it overcomes the weight and transforms the matter, to such a degree that it has an excess. Cattle are creatures with something to *give*.

The scorpion is the creature with the driest constitution of all the creatures of the zodiac. It has an primitive digestive system. On the other hand, for such a relatively simple creature, its eyes are extremely well developed.

The bull has a powerful circulation and the blood circulates from the back to the front. Once the animal is at rest, the blood flows through the head to the horns, and from there it is recirculated. When it becomes angry, the circulation is stronger than ever. This results in a tremendous drive to butt with its horns, but at the same time it disturbs the calm functioning of the senses. In general, the eye, which is the conscious sensory organ in humans, and which owes its great clarity to its separation from the other life processes, does not play a major role in cattle. The ear is better developed, but the most powerful sense which is most closely related to metabolism, is the sense of smell.

In the scorpion the tail is highly developed, and at the end of the tail is the power centre of the sting. There is a movement from the front to the back which is developed in the urge to sting.

An abundance of life forces circulates the bull's blood towards the head, while the scorpion's death forces flow out through its tail. It is hardly surprising that the scorpion, which has a constitutional lack of life force, is cautious, taking hold of its prey with its pincers, in order to keep the victim away from its valuable head.

There is a great difference between a creature which meets its opponent literally head on and powerfully tries to force him aside, and a creature which crawls out of a hidden corner with its fatal weapon, cautiously feels its way about until it locates a weak spot and then strikes the deadly blow with the minimum of effort.

The bull represents an aspect of the burgeoning of spring. Its strength and its powerful outward movements reveal something of the irrepressible rising of the sun, and the continuing distancing of the sun and the earth during this season.

The scorpion represents the desiccated death process which take place in the autumn. Like the autumn sun, it is completely in the grip of darkness and heaviness.

There is an intriguing tradition which is of great significance in revealing the deeper nature of man's essence. The image of the scorpion is sometimes also seen as the image of the eagle.

The eagle

Of all the signs of the zodiac, the eagle is characterized by the fact that it can fly high and wide above the earth. It is carried by forces which are of little importance to the others and which are totally nonexistent in relation to the bull.

When the sun sets in the evening with a golden glow over the crude and jagged mountain tops, the eagle breaks all its earthly ties and surrenders to flight into the highest regions. It stretches its wings until they are spread so widely that they almost seem to break with the tension. Then it glides up high, seemingly without any effort, describing giant circles. The powerful figure of the bird is clearly silhouetted, dark against the radiant sky, even when the evening rays burnish its plumage with a deep golden brown glow. It can go on rising like this forever, until the giant creature is hardly more than a speck in the distance.

When the eagle lands on the ground and tries to walk, it becomes exceptionally awkward; it will quickly rise again, and it is clear that the creature is not at home on the earth.

But then we can see it resting in a high place, gripping a lonely crag with its claws, with the fierce eyes in its dry, sharp head able to see for miles. The powerful drive which carries it away from the earth is expressed in its entire form, its upright posture and markedly upward-pointing shoulders and wings. When it finally stretches out its wings to take off, it makes tremendous movements aimed at the widths of the world. With these giant gestures it is greeting the stars.

When a pair of eagles hunt early in the morning, they glide down from their high eyrie and wing their way down hills and through valleys. They cover vast distances, and with their eagle eyes they see everything that moves below.

When an eagle sees a small animal scurrying away, it

undergoes a terrifying change. The wings are folded tight against the body and pointed back, and then the bird plummets to the earth with its feathers rippling, until it seizes its victim, talons outspread. Its talons tear into the fleece and its sharp beak rips at the head and eyes of its prey until there is no life left. Then it stands proudly for a moment, its neck held forward, the neck feathers pointing downwards, jubilantly uttering its cry of victory. An incredible concentration is required for this wild chase.

Then the eagle rises up again, beating its wings heavily and carrying its load to a high and lonely spot. It tears meat off its prey piece by piece, starting at the head, and slowly gorges itself.

It is clear that the eagle's element is the wide open space. Landing on the ground is rather like a visit which requires an effort. So it hauls its prey back up to the heights as quickly as possible. The eagle's hunting is more of a theft than that of the lion, for it enters alien territory and then carries off its booty to its own territory.

Throughout its existence the eagle lives with the forces of death and destruction. In the eyrie high up in the craggy heights, the female often lays several eggs. As soon as the ugly naked eglets crawl out of their shells, the parents bring dead animals to the nest. These are greedily devoured, but quite a few remains are left lying around, so that there is a horrible putrid atmosphere. As soon as one of the young has become the strongest, it attacks and kills the others. It tries to push them out of the nest. In the end, only one of the young ever survives.

As the young bird grows older, the parent birds leave it alone for longer periods, and sometimes it is many days before they bring fresh food. After a few months it takes its first flight, and then its life of wandering continues for several years. In fact, the whole life of the eagle is characterized by its solitary existence and loneliness, with the exception of the loyalty which binds the pairs together for many years.

The eagle's relation to the earth is similar to that of its

physiology. It adopts an attitude of extreme reticence towards both the earth and its own body. Only a small part of its body has blood flowing through it. Most of the body is taken up with warm air and feathers. In fact, the bird contains a number of large air pockets, which means that a powerful air current passes back and forth through the lungs, especially during flight. The lungs are connected to the air spaces in the hollow bones. Further out, the feathers also retain a substantial layer of air. The surface area of the entire creature is greatly increased by the large flight feathers, and again, this is particularly the case during flight.

The eagle and the bull

We have mentioned the contrast between lightness and heaviness, and in this respect the eagle can be characterized as a creature whose whole life and endeavours are aimed at the heights, the distance and the rarefied nature of light. No aspect of its flight points to the depths. The legs are drawn in and the talons contracted. As it glides through the air it forms a powerful plane at right angles to the earth; the beating of its wings indicates the infinite distances of the widths of the earth. Of course, even the eagle's body has a material nature, and much of it is composed of hard, earthly matter, but the eagle lives as though it would like to be permanently drawn away from the earth by higher forces.

How can a creature inhabit a certain region in a harmonious way? It does this by becoming part of the interplay of forces in this region, and allowing these to form him. The eagle raises a burden of earthly matter into an area where it does not belong. It does this by assuming a flat, radiating form in flight, its feathers extending into a fine interplay of lines, points and sharp angles.

This is one of the basic principles of nature: whenever solid matter is influenced by the creative force of light, this gives rise to sharp, fine, radiant forms, often accompanied by a linear structure.

The bull and the eagle have scarcely a line in common; the bull's legs are supporting pillars which point towards the earth and its whole body is a dense compact mass of solid substance.

Through its senses the eagle is also strongly oriented towards the widths of light. Everything on earth can be seen from the height at which it flies; something which seems large to us is only a speck to the eagle in a distant plane below. Nevertheless, it is able to focus on a single object with unusual concentration. The eagle's sense of balance and of movement is also unusually powerful. It has an excellent sense of hearing, though this is secondary to its sight. Thus the eagle can be characterized by an unusually alert nervous and sensory experience, aimed at the periphery. On the other hand, the senses which are used to explore the hidden forces of matter, those of smell and taste, are poorly developed.

When we compare this with the cow, it is clear that the latter has little awareness of light, though it has a strong relationship with the deeper quality of matter. The cow uses its sense of smell to distinguish poisonous crops, and is even able to find its own herbal remedies.

The eagle is very inactive in terms of metabolic processes. It starts these processes by killing prey that is easy to digest. The feathers consist of discharged dead matter, and are hardly significant for other organisms. Its faeces have a high mineral content. Even its body is not left to others, for there are not really any creatures which are able to catch and kill it, and it lives to a relatively great age.

In this way it contributes very little to the life processes of nature as a whole. It does contribute to the breakdown of living matter in nature, but it does little for its creation. It *takes* a great deal, and *gives* very little in life.

The bull contrasted with scorpion and eagle

The spring sun moves further and further away from the earth, but as it does so, it has a stronger regulatory effect on matter, drawing it up in the form of plants. The bull is oriented towards the solid matter of plants as they rise up out of the earth, and in this way raises up matter even further in the structure of its powerful body. Springtime, as well as the cow's constitution, is characterized by the raising of matter into the sphere of the cosmic forces of growth and the profound effect of the forces of growth on matter.

The autumn sun sinks deeper and deeper below the earth, allowing solid matter increasingly to escape the grasp of its life forces. Autumn time is characterized by the loss of matter from the sphere of life into the purely mineral sphere, and by the separation of life forces from matter. There is a tremendous decomposition, a form of analysis, while the spring brings about a powerful synthesis. The eagle and the scorpion both take whole animals to break down and reduce to dead excretory products. Their life is based on tearing matter from the cosmic life process.

The scorpion contrasted with the eagle

In many respects scorpion and eagle correspond. They are outwardly dry and arid. Their limbs are withered. The eagle holds its prey at a distance, just like the scorpion. This is different from the lion, which throws itself at its prey with its whole body, engulfing it. It is also significant that both the scorpian and the eagle use spiked points which are a characteristic feature. In the eagle the beak ends in a razor-sharp point, and it can never hide its talons like other predators. In both these respects they are diametrically opposed to the bull. However, there are also great differences between them. While scorpions are creatures which crawl close to the earth, the eagle lives on an elevated plane.

The effect of vigorous life forces can be studied in the bull and cow, while the eagle and the scorpion demonstrate the possibilities of the forces of death in a very different way.

Leo

Between July 23 and August 24 the sun is still very high, but its arc is descending at an increasing rate. It shines with tremendous strength, but is no longer able to awaken new life from the earth. Its light abates so that the earth bathes in a strong summer glow. All around one can see the life processes being brought to an end. It is the time at which the fruits and seeds become ripe in a sultry atmosphere of heat.

The lion inhabits regions on earth where the strength of the sun makes it impossible for trees to flourish, in the tropical savannah. In Africa there are huge plains of grass with occasional trees or clumps of trees. Zebras and ostriches, giraffes and countless antelope graze there together. The bristly gnus flee from their attacker, making the most peculiar leaps. At night one is woken up by the dreadful howling of hyenas which wander about in their grubby coats enjoying their stinking prey. These areas are rich in wild animals, an ideal region for hunting big game.

In the middle of all this wealth, where nature reaches a climax in the creation of many different species, the lion inhabits a worthy environment. It does not like to attack small animals. It also lives on big game, and is prepared to go through tension and combat in order to gain its food. It prefers to attack zebras which are larger and much faster than itself, and are able to defend themselves with great strength.

At night there is often a lot of noise in the wilderness, but the lion rises above it. When it roars and growls, its head pointing to the earth, it is as though the whole area falls silent. There is hardly another creature on earth which produces such a powerful noise.

While hunting, the lion is silent. The strong animal with its yellowish brown coat creeps quietly through the night. It lies in ambush on one of the well-trodden tracks leading to the watering holes. A herd of antelope approaches with pricked ears, sniffing carefully. Suddenly there is a flurry and a few tremendous leaps, and the leading antelope is brought down as though struck by lightning. There it lies, while the lion's powerful body seems glued to it, breaking the neck of its prey with a powerful thrust of the paw, and then beginning to bite, still growling. Usually the prey is dragged off to some distance away and then devoured, while the lion continues to growl passionately.

After its meal, the lion takes a rest. It lies as still as a stone with its proud head and flaming mane, its keen gaze raised. The satiated lion is a perfect symbol of a good balance in the self and an agreeable awareness of one's own strength. Sometimes the lion is seen by day, standing on a small outcrop in the middle of its territory, as though surveying its subjects.

The lion seeks out situations which involve great tension and demand skill in combat. It is repeatedly roused by violent emotions, but always comes to rest in perfect peace. It is self-assured, even in the heaviest battle. It is always in control, and always victorious. In most cases predatory activities turn animals into unpleasant repulsive creatures, but the lion is a noble and dignified predator.

Aquarius

Between January 21 and February 19 the sun is still largely below the earth but it rises up at an accelerating rate. It is now actively developing its own nature of light and height. It is precisely against the background of darkness which predominates in winter, that the importance of the sun's nature can really be recognized. As it rises, it also draws up the life forces into hidden areas. As soon as circumstances are at all favourable, all sorts of plants start to appear.

In the signs of the zodiac Aquarius represents man living amongst the animals and yet in contrast with them. Goethe characterized the human form by comparing it with that of animals. Such thoughts are only now being generally rediscovered following more than a century of forgetting the difference between humankind and animals. These words, written at a relatively young age, show Goethe's genius for understanding the world.

> The different order of humans form the animals can be seen in the skeleton. How our head sits on the spine and the force of life. The whole form is a pillar for the dome which is a reflection of the heavens. How our skull is arched like the sky above us to allow the pure image of the eternal spheres circle within it. How the vessel of the brain is the largest part of the head. How through the jaws all emotions rise and fall and collect on the lips. How the eye, the most expressive of all organs needs not words, but tender loving devotion, or the grim concentration of the cheeks, and all the gradations between to be expressed, nay only to stammer, what passes through the inmost depths of humanity!

> And how the structure of the animal is just the opposite. The head is only attached to the back. The brain, the end of the spinal cord, has no more size than is necessary to fulfil the compulsions of its life and to lead a creature living in the moment of the senses. Though we cannot straight away deny them memory and reasoned decision, so the latter, I would say, lies in the first place in the senses and springs from the impulses of the moment and the imbalance of this or that object.

> Nose and mouth are the most obvious part of

the head, and are there to sniff, chew, and swal-
low. The muscles are flat and tense, covered by a
rough skin incapable of any pure expression.*

Imagine a naked figure of a man and compare it, perhaps even with a lion. This must produce a powerful
impression if we view it without preconceptions. The figure
of a man is noble and elevated, and Goethe used the right
words when he referred to a pillar and a dome. Man is the
only spiritual being which stands completely upright.
Every animal's body bends or curves in some way, no
matter how it raises itself up. Man is the only creature
that fully accepts the structure of the world. With his legs
he points down to heaviness, so that he is all the more able
to oppose this force. Because of the shape of his head he is
able to face in all directions. He is wholly in harmony with
the rarefied nature of the world of light, and yet he is at
the same time a dense creature of the earth. His whole
body and locomotion is such that his head is raised above
the nether regions as far as possible, and liberated as
much as possible from contact with other earthly matter.
The human head consists of solid earthly matter which is
carried as though it is on the way to becoming a celestial
body.

It is hardly surprising that a creature with this structure
is the only spiritual being on earth. What other dwelling
place could house the spirit, which is all-embracing and all-
pervasive, than this figure which forms a harmonious part
of the world? One could not think of a simpler symbol for
this aspect of the human figure than the single water
pitcher that stands upright next to Aquarius. The water
pitcher is an earthly artefact with an opening at the top to
receive something from above, just as the human body is
open to the spirit.

Thus we can also understand that there is a connection
between the human figure and the depths of the winter

* from 'Eingang,' *Physiognomische Fragmenten* in Goethe's *Naturwissen-
schaftliche Schriften*, Vol.II).

season. In the sun-earth constellation there is a dynamic process, as in man when he is standing upright. In order to raise his head towards the world of light he has to reject the earth and at the same time place himself fully in its interplay of forces. The sun in winter, as well as the real human at this stage, is a creature of light bound to the earth, but endeavouring to rise above it to express its true nature.

Other profound insights can be gained by comparing the human hand with the limbs of animals.* In all the animals the limbs have become tools, paws for walking, webbed feet for swimming, wings or talons. In every animal the structure of the leg depends on its task in relation to a particular field. In other respects it is of little use. It always develops in a very one-sided fashion. Animals' paws can always be seen to be derived from the human hand, but never the other way round. Usually it is clear that one of the aspects of the hand is strongly pronounced, while others disappear. The wing of a bird is like a highly evolved index finger, a horse's hoof is like a middle finger on its own. In a human hand all the aspects have been retained and are in equilibrium. The result is that the hand is not connected with any particular area, but conversely it is more or less useful in the most diverse fields. This brings us to a basic law of human development, in which everything depends on holding back. Man must constantly suppress the danger of one-sided development, of becoming an animal.

We can also see how an animal's paw is completely integrated into natural life. An animal can only use its paws in connection with its own life functions or caring for its offspring. A similar rule applies to the head of an animal. In contrast, man is able to liberate his hands from such bonds. He is able to use his hands to serve his fellow creatures, or for higher spiritual tasks.

---

* See *Man and Animal* by Hermann Poppelbaum (Anthroposophical Publishing Co, London 1960).

Ultimately the hand is the central organ in shaping events, so that the earth can be renewed and transformed. Even the greatest spiritual force can have no effect in transforming the earth if man does not put his hand to it.

The hand can open to give or receive without any trace of desire. When it serves its true purpose, it is used for the highest creative work. But the hand can also become tightly convulsed in order to accumulate possessions. In this case it becomes a deadly claw.

This brings us to an understanding of the pitcher next to Aquarius. It lies on its side with water flowing out. The Latin word *Aquarius* means water carrier. It is not difficult to imagine what water means to man and the world in hot dry regions. It is only there that it is truly appreciated as a life-giving element which restores health. It emanates freshness and purity. The ideal image of the human being is of a bringer of life, awakening new vitality in the dead earth.

Aquarius and Leo

It is possible to gain significant insights by comparing in detail the lion with man. The lion expresses its physical strength to its surroundings in every respect. It expresses it in its flaming mane, its thundering roar, which shakes the whole vicinity, its heavy claws which have become awesome weapons, the abyss of its maw, surrounded by the shining white teeth pointing inwards like sabres. Even the end of its tail is armoured with a horny tip. The lion is a creature in which all the organs have evolved for the purpose of attack and combat. Its whole being is raised to greatness, though always at the expense of others.

In comparison, the human figure is movingly delicate and frail. A man who goes into nature without any tools or artefacts would not survive long. His sensitive skin is not really strong enough to enclose and protect the body. The fact that the organization of the human body does not simply disintegrate, and that it is not in constant mortal danger, is due more to the singular process of the clotting of the blood than to the skin. In comparison with the hides or armour of animals, it is clear that the separation between man and his environment is extremely small.

The lion is like the summer sun, shining powerfully from above, and violently casting itself down on to events on earth with its movement.

Man is like the winter sun: his essence is housed in concealed depths, and he transforms and renews the world from inside himself.

The true greatness of man does not lie in his external strength or in the violent physical control of the material world. If his physical development is promoted primarily and in a one-sided way, his spirit is increasingly repressed. It is only really clear to what extent man's spirit can be truly expressed through restraint when the human hand is compared to a lion's claw, and the expressions of each of these is examined. Although man is every bit as much a king in his field as the lion is, and even greater, still it may be said of man: 'His kingdom is not of this world.'

In man the spiritual kingdom becomes manifest. All other creatures are created out of this, so he is familiar with their origin. In him, the meaning of their existence is explained. Therefore how could his activities in the external world ever be anything other than assistance and a blessing for others? Their interests are also his own, for their essence lives in him as his most personal aspect. A man true to his nature will never be hostile towards any other creature. He does not enter into combat or suppress others, for he encompasses all other creatures with his conscious inner being.

This also explains how we cannot think of the lion without seeing the blood flowing from its claws. The lion saps the life force of other creatures.

In contrast, we see how man can help and cure the wounded, and this is an image which reveals the highest possible achievements on earth, far transcending the animal aspect. The hands of true man constantly emanate a current of healing life force.

As he restrains the tendency for far-reaching specialization at every point of his development, man retains a reserve of growth force. It is this force which he makes available to others.

Rudolf Steiner once pointed out that pain signifies something much worse for the higher animals than it does for humans. An animal lives as a pure soul creature, without suppressing its feelings in any way, and is completely taken up by them. As spiritual beings, humans bear something within them which transcends the emotions of the soul. To some extent they can even be an observer of the worst things which befall them.

A suffering animal *is* suffering. It is not able to assimilate this suffering. Only humans know the harvest of suffering. They are all too familiar with the path through the valley of tears, but the deeper they descend, the higher they will climb up the mountain path of personal development.

An animal seeks a sense of well-being in everything it does. These expressions of well-being are found to the greatest extent in the lion. Only humans are familiar with the actions which transcend physical pleasure. They are familiar with great renunciation *vis-à-vis* everything provided by the world. They are able to say 'No' to many things to which an animal says 'Yes' with its whole being.

Again we return to the relation with the cosmic constellation. The lion shows us a particular side of the animal world in the highest degree: an unreserved surrender to the environment and the search for well-being. In this way we see how the sun reveals the least restraint in the summer and casts itself down on earth to the greatest extent.

On the other hand, the sun in winter is actively renewing itself and rising up after passing through darkness. Outwardly it is still extremely restrained, although it is actively aiming for the greatest height. In the same way we can feel sure that as a human has risen higher, he or she has also descended deeper into the dark abyss of sorrow.

The blessed extensive powers of a truly developed human are dressed in sorrow, and the blessing of the light in spring is all the greater because it was born in darkness.

The deepest descent is represented by the centaur, man bound to an animal. There is only one possible image for the sun rising, for its liberation from its prison constituted by the earth and darkness, for the realization of its true nature — this is the image of man himself.

Sagittarius

Sagittarius is the sign through which the sun passes between November 23 and December 22. At the end of the November the sun's arc has sunk down below the earth, and still it sinks down even further every night and rises less during the day. However, the rate of this change gradually decreases until it finally comes to a standstill before its deepest position. We see how at this time the sun is most closely linked to darkness and heaviness, but also how it powerfully opposes a further surrender to the depths. It is as though it is concentrating on its imminent nature of light, and is therefore achieving the greatest tension with the forces of depth.

The image of the centaur with his bow and arrow appears to us in this conjunction. This is a creature in which the higher rises above the lower, without being able to free itself. It is a creature which is full of inner turmoil because the higher aspect is bound to an extremely violent lower nature.

There was a time — though this was long ago — when Sagittarius was seen as a creature full of elevated wisdom as well as an eminent teacher. The Greeks called him Chiron, and considered him to be the teacher of all their mythological heroes and demigods.

However, since that time a great deal has changed. A

variety of symptoms suggest that Sagittarius should be viewed as being related to all sorts of dark and dramatic problems. But in order to acquire a precise picture of this image, we should first consider the life of the horse.

Wild horses are wonderful fiery creatures. Usually they live in large groups divided into many smaller herds, each consisting of a number of mares with their foals, and one stallion. They inhabit, above all, wild treeless steppes, enormous plains with endless horizons. They are extremely lively. They will run for hours every day for the pure joy of movement, thundering on the ground with their hooves, snorting with flared nostrils, manes and tails swishing wildly, whipped up by the driving wind.

When they encounter something strange on their path, they swerve and simply gallop past. They stand still at a distance to take a curious look, heads raised high, but then a shock passes through them and they take off in a flying gallop.

Sometimes a whole herd of horses will stampede. They gallop on as though whipped along, leaving clouds of dust behind them. The whole earth trembles with the thundering of their hooves. They trample everything that comes in their way, and they are so blinded by their tremendous fear that they are capable of crashing into an abyss.

Woe to any creature that dares to attack a herd of wild horses. The stallions are sure enough of their power and agility that they even try to surround bloodthirsty packs of wolves, battering them with their sharp fore hooves.

There is a dreadful fight amongst the stallions for the mares. A lonely stallion can be seen standing on an outcrop, its head and flaming eyes raised high, its tail stretched out like a flag. When it spies a herd, it gallops forth to challenge the leader; close to the enemy, it swings round at full speed and kicks up with its back legs, as quick as lightning. Then the two stallions rear up against each other, tearing with their teeth, kicking and beating with their hooves until one finally clears the field. In this way horses can be seen as the most violent and passionate of creatures.

Horses can be classified as ungulates. This means that four of the toes have disappeared from the foot, leaving only the middle toe which carries the heavy hoof. Horses have perfect feet for running, but this foot is also the furthest removed from the human hand. One cannot imagine a more hardened and one-sided foot.

When horses run past, they shake the ground more than any other creatures. They seem to pound the earth. However, this is only possible because the horse's foot ends in a clod of earth, its heavy hoof. None of the higher animals is more bound to the earth by its legs than the horse.

As for the centaur: this is a creature in which man is bound to his passionate tumultuous animal spirit. The upper half is upright and has the power of a human mind. In this way it can direct the violent power below, though it is unable to suppress it. The centaur should not be represented as it was by the Greeks. They were barely able to express any other aspect than its beauty and transcendent nature. Böcklin's *Kentaurenkampf* gives a much better impression. It shows these human horses of gigantic stature engaged in the most violent battle. The bodies of the horses are heavy and swollen like carthorses, while the human bodies are rough and strong and their faces distorted. The harmony of the face is also distorted; the foreheads are low and receding, the noses flattened, the chins are small.

Until now we have described the creatures and sensed something of their deeper nature from their appearance and lifestyle. However, here we must develop a greater skill and describe a creature which does not exist in the natural world. We must empathise with this creature to such an extent that it does not just appear before our imagination as though we are observing it with our senses; we must also deduce its whole nature from its behaviour and the environment in which it belongs. This may seem a hopeless task. And yet if there is any consistency in the relationship between the deeper nature of living creatures and their outward appearance, it must be possible.

Our usual train of thought comes up against a wall, but then we do not even penetrate the depths of familiar natural creatures. We will only be able to break through if we practise our artistic skills to such an extent that we are able to identify with the great creative processes on which natural creatures are based. It is only then that we will succeed in treating mythological creatures in such a way that they live a natural life. Our imagination will have to show us the way towards new realms.

Before further examining the image of Sagittarius let us take a look at Gemini, the twins, for it is the polarity between these two images that gives us a key to grasping their nature.

Gemini

From May 22 to June 22 the sun's arc is raised high up above the earth and continues to rise every day. Every day it increases; every night it sinks less far into the dark. Nothing remains of the tremendous tensions and immeasurable force which developed during the winter. The powerful rising movement increasingly becomes a time of rest in the heights. The events in the natural world increasingly take place in an atmosphere of light. Together with this the life of plants and animals develops to a high degree. Much of what remained concealed within or in darkness before is now manifest to the eye and to the senses in general. It is a time of great revelations.

Twins are an image of the child. When the tradition of the Nativity describes the baby lying between the ox and the ass, this is a reference to the image of twins, for it falls between the image of the bull or the ox and the image of the crab which was also called the ass in the past.

Children have a particular environment just as animals do. Wherever there are children it is as though everything lights up and becomes clear, as though the world is glorified by the wonderful glow of the sun. This immediately creates the impression of the sunny period of Gemini from the essence of a child.

Imagine on a sunny clear summer's day two merry children on a grassy field bedecked with flowers, perhaps with a slight rise in the middle, being left alone to gambol about quite freely. If our soul is opened wide to catch all the sounds of joy, all the happy and playful movements, we would come to realize that with their playful gambolling, children reenact paradise on earth. Flowers, sunlight and butterflies form the appropriate setting for Gemini.

Children also have a very different side. When they are in pain, or cannot succeed in doing something which they have set out to achieve, they can be so downcast with sorrow that it seems they will never recover. However, in a healthy child joy far outweighs sorrow.

This also applies to the sun in the month of June: it sets every night as though descending to the depths of the earth, but in fact this is incidental, for it is a rising creature which inhabits the heavens.

To our way of thinking every child is a magician. As an adult, we can only smile in awe when we see children working with their hands. One can admire their seriousness and share their joy. Everything the child picks up turns into something different, something better. A piece of wood turns into a doll, the stake from a fence into a horse.

When we look back at ourselves with honesty, we feel a deep sense of melancholy about our loss. What happened to all that wealth, all that purity? Our actions have become impoverished, for life forces us to direct all our actions on the basis of serious considerations. We are bowed down by the feeling of all the urges within us. We should like to raise ourselves up to become liberated creatures, and to become powerful, but our passions break down so much of this feeling in us. Why is it that all this richness constantly flows from a child? One of Rudolf Steiner's central teachings in connection with human development casts light on this. The child's whole constitution is completely different in every sense from that of an adult. We can see how the personality awakes in the course of life, and how this has a particular disposition. However, we rarely ask how the forces of this personality operated before they became accessible to consciousness. Rudolf Steiner pointed out that in early childhood these forces were aimed in particular at building up a physical organization. First, the vehicle for the personality must be forged so that later it is available for conscious use. At the time we are unaware of this activity because our consciousness is not ready to partake in a higher wisdom which works in the creation of our body. It is the higher spirit of the developing human being which prepares the body, but its activities are completely guided by higher spiritual powers. The higher spirit is still entirely embedded in the spiritual world of light, where its origins lie. First, it acts on the physical organization from outside as it were. Gradually it enters more and more and looks to the outside world with the help of its own creation, through the body. This development entails a gradual separation from the higher powers, and in many respects forms a bond with a lower aspect. However, one of the greatest human attributes, independence, and the potential for freedom, depends on this process, although man pays for this with the profound tragedy of cosmic loneliness.

Gemini and Sagittarius

We have seen how the position of sun and earth in the period of Gemini is comparable to the character of a child. The sun, when it is deeply submerged in the earth, and the far-reaching separation from the heights which occurs in the period of Sagittarius, is comparable with an adult mentality, especially that of a male. Possibly there is no aspect which reveals the tragic side of earthly existence so deeply. Children see adults as an ideal. They wish to imitate adults, follow them and learn from them. They wish to be just the same so that they can really work and achieve great things. But once they have achieved this, they realize that they have lost almost everything that once gave them joy and richness. Then the child becomes an ideal to the adult.

Again, there is a revealing contrast between the child's hand and the horse's hoof, or between the child's hands and the rough fists drawing the fatal bow. The child's hand cannot destroy or injure; in their games children can only enrich the world and make it flourish. Children have the key to the future which we have lost, but they lack the power to use it, a power which we do have.

How sad that the rich world created in a child's play is so transient. However, when we encounter this tragedy we learn to understand its deeper meaning. A child's game is not reality; it is merely a sunny reflection of the creative activity of higher powers working on his constitution. Let us be grateful to these divine powers for at least giving us this message of their existence and their working on our dark path. Why should we not use all the powers we have to achieve the ideal displayed before us by the child? In fact Schiller, who suffered immeasurably under the bonds of earthly existence, gave us the play of the child as an example. In his *Letters on the Aesthetic Education of Mankind* he referred to two forces which bind man, the urge for form, *Formtrieb,* and the urge for matter, *Stofftrieb,* but he also mentioned a third force which gave him freedom in creation, the urge for play, *Spieltrieb.*

This is a general problem experienced by everyone. It is expressed in the most extreme terms in the images of Gemini and Sagittarius. In the former we find supernatural lightness, airiness and joy, while in Sagittarius there is enormous strength which is forcefully aimed at particular goals, so that it becomes particularly effective. However, Sagittarius is shrouded in a dark mood. To approach him one must suffer extreme pain, and even great danger.

There is a great deal to be learnt about the character of Sagittarius from the way in which he uses his bow. First, it is fully drawn by pulling back the bowstring, then released so that it springs back and all the force which is liberated is transmitted in the arrow, which is accurately aimed and flies into the distance, finally hitting a single carefully selected spot with all the pent-up force.

The arrow shooting through space is an appropriate image for the movement of the sun on a December day. As it moves down, there is a surrender to the tense grasp of deep forces, followed by an upward movement which does describe a low arc above the earth, although the emphasis is on an imminent descent and return to the depths.

The daily movement of the sun in the month of June is like a game with a golden ball. It rises high up into the air and then descends only to spring up again from the depths. The whole of life is like this for the twins. They draw up everything they encounter, so that it shines brilliantly in the light and freedom of the higher regions, or even in the realm of illusions.

Sagittarius is always concerned with deep forces by summoning violent tensions, or by directing events towards a specific goal. He is deeply concentrated, focused and bound to the depths. Just as the strength of his hands is concentrated in the force of the tip of the arrow, all the might of the horse's legs is focused in a single hoof.

In this way the image of the centaur comes alive.

He stands at the edge of the wood, a mighty figure, his rough torso rising above the body of the horse. His gaze directed far into the distance, hardly noticing what is nearby. A deer bounds by, and he follows it. He leaps forward with his tall body bent back, and rushes on chasing the fleeing prey. We can hear the earth thunder under the pounding of his hooves. No matter how fast the deer may run, whipped on by the fear of death, Sagittarius will catch up, shooting it to the ground with his sharp arrow.

Of all other creatures of the zodiac, he is the strongest, and unconquerable. It is only himself that he cannot overcome. Often he feels tired of the chase and the struggle. The human in him awakes and wishes to subdue the animal in him, making it rest, so liberating his human self. A noble look briefly passes over his distorted features, but then the dreadful suffering of writhing passions gains the upper hand again. He stamps his hooves wildly and rears up. The human strains to pull free, but remains shackled. He becomes exhausted and seems smaller, even impotent. One is tempted to approach him, catch him and tame him. Do not do so, for he will rise up like a giant and smash everything in his path with titanic strength.

Virgo

Between August 24 and September 24 the sun has long passed its zenith. The great unfolding of heat after the beginning of the descent, which had signified an increase in its power, has passed. The whole of nature is affected by a process of cooling, and falls silent. The first transparent mornings of autumn are at hand. As the sun is now setting almost at its fastest rate, the emphasis every day is increasingly on the sunset, when the huge body of light sinks down, shining gold, into the lap of the earth's darkness. The plant world starts to withdraw into buds, seeds, root stocks etc. The fine veils of mist, which are a common feature of this period, are a characteristic phenomenon.

How can one describe Virgo? The secret lies in the mystery of the virgin which cannot be approached. As soon as it is touched, it no longer exists. It evokes a deep sense of awe, but also indicates that we should withdraw to a respectful distance.

Might it be different if one first became a child? Then one would feel her intimate gaze resting upon one. One would be borne and enveloped as if by a heaven on earth.

We have encountered human figures four times in the

signs of the zodiac, and every time the emphasis has been on a completely different aspect of human existence. This time the image refers to the highest aspect of the female nature.

Virgo is the only figure in the signs of the classic zodiac which is depicted clothed. This exception indicates a characteristic aspect of this sign. In this case, the capacity for being warmly clad, and for protecting oneself from the rough, impure touch of the environment is important. We should imagine Virgo as a creature whose attention is above all focused inwards, and who shuts off the outside world to a great extent. Nevertheless, she is not completely withdrawn and inaccessible. She also possesses an unusual capacity for surrender and openness. This applies particularly in relation to the child, which has not yet developed any earthly qualities, but holds within it the purest heavenly forces. The character of Virgo rejects the dark forces of earth and turns to heavenly forces, even when these are reflected in the environment on earth.

The notion of a woman expecting a child teaches us a great deal about this image. Her body protects and envelops, and above all, retires to allow the new to develop. The child makes use of the opportunity which she provides.

However we approach her, Virgo always suggests the highest qualities. She never develops in a self-willed way, but is always prepared to give of herself. Thus she creates areas where the highest and purest forces can develop, even in rough, downward-pulling surroundings. She is a shining celestial island in the middle of the dark environment of the earth.

Pisces

From February 19 to March 21 the sun has long passed its nadir. The very cold period which expresses the effect of earthly forces drawing downwards has also passed. It is now rising up almost at its fastest rate, so that the light can be powerfully liberated from the darkness. The same process is expressed in a very pure way in the growth of trees and bushes. Their buds start to swell and many green tips push aside the dark bud scales.

Pisces and Cancer are the only creatures in the signs of the zodiac which live in water. The environment plays a very different role for a water creature than it does for a land animal. A land animal is supported by the earth and raises itself up into the rarefied atmosphere of the heavens. It is supported by the hard earth which constantly pulls it downwards, and the air which is always prepared to draw back and make room becomes its real environment. A water creature is carried — as well as enclosed — by its environment to a greater extent.

As we shall see, the crab seeks to be enclosed by water, and even more, it seeks to be supported and protected by the solid earth.

Typical fish behave as though they wish to free themselves from their environment. They can often be seen arcing out of the water. They manage to save themselves, especially when they are being pursued by other creatures in the depths, by leaping into the realms of light above, but then they have to return to the depths. Even when there is no threat at all, the fish can never find any peace or support. It is constantly pushing the water behind it aside with its caudal fin in order to propel itself forward. It constantly frees itself from the water which happens to surround it, but then finds itself in another watery environment. It is so strongly directed at what is ahead of it that it incessantly gulps it in and lets it flow behind it through its gills.

In man, respiration goes in and out, so that the environment is alternately taken in and then expelled. The fish merely seems to 'breathe in.' It is continuously linked to the world ahead, and never rejects it. The whole shape of the fish is attuned to gliding forwards in close contact with the environment. Its body streams back through the fins and tail. If we compare the form of the fins with the veils worn by Virgo, we note that while a veil is wound around the body enclosing it, a fin is a part of the body aimed at the environment.

One of the characteristic features of the fish is its inability to hold back and maintain a distance from its environment. While its whole form and movement express an enormous surrender to the environment, the fish's head reveals a different tendency. The head contains the crack of the mouth, the nostrils, the eyes with circles around them, and the markings on the operculum and gill slits. This tendency indicates something of its own formation and the beginning of a separation from the environment. Because of the pectoral fins just behind the head, the fish has a slight capacity for restraint. These fins can be used to slow down, and can even allow the fish to move backwards.

The description given above — the bonds from which the creature is trying to liberate itself, its attempts to raise itself up into the upper reaches, its movement into the area ahead which is the area of light before its eyes, the pushing back of the water surrounding it into the dark world behind — reflects the arrangement of the earth-sun constellation at the beginning of March.

One of the most remarkable characteristics of fish is their capacity to reflect the environment. I believe that there are hardly any other creatures which are able to do this to the same extent. The silvery scales of the fish always shine with the colour of the objects it is swimming past. Thus the interaction with the environment is so strong that it leaves its imprint on the fish in a permanent exchange. This not only occurs as a result of reflection, for even the lightest hints of its own colour, such as the darker shade of the back, vary depending on the light or darkness in the environment.

The reproduction of fish is also characteristic. In many cases the eggs and the seed are dispersed into the water and the eggs are fertilized in the environment. Because of this, a single female will produce enormous numbers of eggs. Five hundred thousand eggs is by no means unusual for one fish. Bearing in mind that on average only two eggs from every female develop into fully grown fish, it becomes clear that the spawning of such a fish is more concerned with feeding other creatures than with its own reproduction. Almost all the eggs and young are devoured.

Earlier we saw that this tremendous drive for expansion which characterizes fish can also be related to the rising sun as it become more and more radiant (see page 27).

A very common process in the animal world, that of the assimilation of one individual by another, is found in fish to a highly developed degree. In the sea a smaller fish is devoured by a larger fish, which is then devoured by an even larger, or sometimes even by a smaller fish. The metabolic processes and the transformation and exchange of matter are therefore unusually strong in fish, and this is reinforced even further by the life that many fish lead in migrating shoals.

Migration is another of the characteristic aspects of fish. Pisces is the only sign of the zodiac with this wanderlust. Many fish migrate a long way from their place of birth and become dispersed over huge areas. It is therefore curious that in order to reproduce, they are able to find their way back to their place of origin with unfailing accuracy. When this happens, the fish — despite having scattered in every direction — reassemble in huge numbers. The life cycles of many species are characterized by this repeated process of expansion and contraction.

So far we have discussed particularly those fish which have retained their simple basic shape. In fact there is an unbelievable variety of shapes which sometimes assume the strangest forms. Of all the animal orders, the greatest variety of shape is found in fish.

A survey of the entire order reveals that there is a tendency in fish to descend down to the darkest depths, and this is where the most obscure demonic monsters in the animal kingdom are found. This again reveals an aspect of the fish's surrender to its environment to such an extent that the creature becomes a reflection of the questionable aspects of the environment. Fish near the surface often shine brilliantly in many colours, and they move with an airy playfulness. Those in the depths are black and have grotesque shapes. Often the whole creature is determined by its tremendously armoured mouth. In all its diversity the fish order is involved in a tremendous drama of light and dark, or lightness and weight.

It is an interesting fact that fish are the only creatures which use electricity as a weapon. Fish that do this include the electric ray and the electric eel. Electricity is a natural force more related to the realms of weight and heaviness (see page 22), and it is characteristic that it is fish which live on the ocean-bed and have surrendered to great weight which use this force, rather than the lighter, more colourful species.

Virgo contrasted with Pisces

The greatest contrast exists between the nature of Virgo and that of Pisces.

Virgo is enveloped by clothes and veils, and with these she repels the influences of the environment. The fish seems almost too naked, and in this respect seems particularly exposed to the environment.

Virgo is wholly concerned with protecting and caring for her inner world. She wishes to retain an absolute purity and clarity. The fish is directed towards the environment to such an extent that it is constantly threatened by malignant forces and downfall, and even by dissolution and decay.

The whole nature of Virgo consists of a tendency to wait and receive, while on the other hand, Pisces incessantly searches and constantly has to liberate itself from the enveloping environment.

If we consider the problem of the curious interaction between Virgo and Pisces, it becomes increasingly clear that she emanates a sort of pure longing and silent expectation. She is unable to do what fish do so easily; that is, go out into the world to search around. She is dependent on what comes to her. If nothing comes, there is a danger of inner aridity, while the problem of Pisces is the reverse. It consists exactly of the lack of what Virgo has in abundance: an inner reserve and serenity. Admittedly fish constantly return from their wanderings to find their place of origin, but shortly afterwards they disperse again. Obviously this is not a deep problem for each individual fish; it only becomes a problem when an aspect of the nature of the fish is imprinted in a human character.

The shape of the fish is so undeveloped that it could be described as a creature still at the seminal stage. Just like a real seed, it is defenceless and is attacked on all sides by hostile and destructive forces. However, it also possesses a drive towards self-realization. Just as Virgo awaits the birth of her child, the drive which is present in Pisces can be compared to the will to be born.

There is an aspect of the earth which forms a strong bond with the sun. The sun is also imperfect and one-sided if it cannot bind itself to the purest aspect of the earth and take up the struggle against the dark. In Virgo we see the image of the earth prepared to receive the sun and germinate everything planted in it. This is also expressed in the plant world, which flourishes in the interaction between the sun and the earth. Wheat is a very clear example of this. The sun touches the earth and the wheat rises up with such utter purity and such nutritious and life-giving force that Christ said of it: 'Take, eat; this is my body.' Often Virgo is depicted with an ear of corn.

However, there is also an aspect of the earth body which constantly lies in ambush for the sun's forces, which paralyses them and kills off their life-giving strength. This is expressed to some extent in an aspect revealed by Pisces. This is why the sun has to raise itself up from the earth every spring and has to escape the dark depths.

Capricorn

During the period of Capricorn, from December 22 to January 21, the sun starts to rise up from its deepest position. Outwardly there is no great change. Outside the cold even increases. However, the descent of the sun has been arrested and it is now followed by a slow but great ascension. Although this transition is hardly noticeable, it is truly tremendous.

Capricorn, the goat, is a creature with an overwhelming desire to seek out the freedom of the heights. You can see it standing on a protruding rocky outcrop, its legs close together and its powerful horns proudly curving back. It looks down into the distant depths of the valley at its feet. Even when surrounded on all sides by free space, when it is in a position which could only hold death if it lost its footing for a single moment, it is still prepared to defy the attacks of storm and thunder, and if necessary, its enemies.

It lives amongst the rugged rocks where the earth element is elevated to the greatest heights and rises up in a rocky dead mass, high above regions full of sweet life. It seeks out this rugged greatness and measures its strength by it. It could be said that the whole environment challenges it to overcome it with all the strength and agility that it can muster.

We need only look at domesticated kids to discover the first early traces of this character. These kids can often be found as high as they can get, even if this is no more than on top of a shed or a hillock. There is also a perversity in their sideways butting leaps, their playful fights, and all their other activities.

Mature goats continue to express a capricious and restless tendency in all their activities and even in their form. While a cow will graze bare whole plains of grass with imperturbable equanimity, goats constantly look for something different as they are feeding. They walk hither and thither, taking a few mouthfuls. They only feel happy with great variety.

Billy goats have a very difficult character. They are strong and sombre lords with a curious askance gaze. Even the smallest challenging movement will arouse their aggression. The goatherd often has to act in an emphatic way, for billy goats do not easily tolerate a power above them, and once they have established a position, they will not relinquish it at any price.

The way in which goats butt each other is remarkable. They rise up on their hind legs and, with the lower jaw held down on the neck and the horns bent forwards, they fiercely butt downwards.

While female goats make a fresh and playful impression, the males have dark traits. They emit a foul odour especially during the mating season. At this time their whole conduct is noticeably tasteless. Even for herd animals, their sexual urge seems unusually pronounced.

The wild mountain goat reveals similar characteristics, but these are raised to a much more elegant style. Usually they live in and near high wooded areas. When they are threatened, they do not seek refuge in the vegetation, but withdraw up into the rocks. They do not seek protection in the environment, but take up the battle with circumstance precisely when there is danger. It is only their agility and ability to leap to places where no other animal can follow them that saves them.

They are creatures with unusual skills and sharp senses. They not only see far into the distance, but as they are leaping about, they can distinguish the smallest ledge that can serve as a support. Their sense of balance is incredible, so that they are perfectly in control in the most impossible situations. They even know how to use their speed to scale rock faces where there is no support at all. There is no question that a creature with this nature would allow itself to be driven out by the winter in the mountains. With its thick coat and heavy layer of fat, it is prepared to defy the worst cold and most severe deprivations. This can be explained, however, by the fact that high up where the wind blows fiercely, the snow is often blown away to reveal what sustinence there is. While food is buried under a thick layer of snow lower down, there may still be some sparse plants to be found higher up.

Cancer

During the period of Cancer, from June 22 to July 23, the sun starts to fall from its highest position. The world is still getting hotter. Outwardly there is little change; for a time there is rest in the heights. In reality the sun is like a ball that has reached its highest point after a strong throw and is now starting to lose height. Before the movement counteracted gravity, now after a slight hesitation, it surrenders to it.

Cancer and Pisces are the only creatures of the zodiac which live in water. The crab lives under the earth's surface, but its whole structure and behaviour also show a strong connection with earthly forces.

Let us look at the crab in front of its retreat, its claws like heavy weapons before it on the sand. Its long antennae carefully feel the sand. On each side of its head, there is a small movement of a limb, keeping respiration moving. Further back, there is a whole series of larger and smaller legs, indistinct in the shadow. The most noticeable feature is the rigid armour, heavily accentuated with sharp edges and spines.

When danger threatens, the crab quickly scuttles back into its hole by moving its wide, flat tail strongly downwards and forwards. Despite its strength, its armour and weapons, it still seeks out the cover and protection of its surroundings.

However, the crab cannot always be so cautious, for it must eat, in fact it likes to eat a lot. So it regularly goes hunting, walking forwards slowly, and, after testing it with its antennae, it takes hold of anything suitable with its pincers. It is not fussy, and will snatch living creatures, dead creatures and even bits of plants.

Then the food has to be transferred to its mouth, and the heavy pincers are not suitable for this. It uses the little pincers on its front claws to pick off small bits and pass them into its mouth.

The crab has an impressive array of equipment: two pairs of antennae, eyes on stalks, a series of mouth cavities, heavy pincers, legs with little pincers and legs without, as well as a whole series of legs for digging itself in. Each of these tools is a variation on a leg. In the crab, even the eye is a variation of a leg.

For the respiration there are two cavities to the side of the body which are covered by a fold in the breastplate, and which contain gills in the form of finely-branched thread-like passages (again appendices of the legs). The water is breathed in through a slit on the back of the breastplate, and streams out in front through an opening next to the head. We described how in fish the respiration was like a process of breathing in only, but for the crab the respiration is a continual out-breathing at the front.

The female freshwater crab protects her eggs underneath the back of her body. When they hatch the young crabs hold on to the mother for some time, with the small legs they have for digging. The mother crab looks after her brood by protecting them underneath the back of her body. This is a highly characteristic gesture of the crab. It is clear that the mother crab temporarily surrenders the reflex for flight, just as the mother scorpion abandons her stinging reflex.

The contrast with fish is interesting: the fish constantly embraces the world in front of it, while rejecting the world behind it, while the crab is extremely cautious with regard to what is ahead, pointing its weapons in this direction, while it blindly escapes into the world behind whenever there is danger in front.

To protect itself further it deposits a thick layer of calcium in the skin. Its whole body, and all its organs with all their large and small protuberances, is surrounded by this hard casing. And yet it has to grow. So every now and again it fasts for a while, allowing its armour plating to become roomier. At the same time, calcium is removed from the skin and stored in a special space in the stomach. Finally a break appears behind the breastplate and the creature wriggles out of its shell taking all its legs and appendages with it. Then it remains concealed for a while, as it cannot move because it lacks firm support. Meanwhile it grows a little and the damaged parts regenerate. Then calcium is again deposited in the skin and the cycle starts all over again.

These peculiar characteristics are appreciated more when they are compared with the opposite sign. Imagine the crab and its lifestyle seen through the eyes of Capricorn!

Again in contrast to the sure-footed mountain goat, the crab has a strange organ of balance. It is an opening containing some grains of sand which opens outwards. Every time the crab sheds its shell, it also loses the skin of this organ and with it the grains of sand for the balance. The crab has to replace these with new grains of sand. There was a scientist who let a crab shed its shell on iron filings. When the process was completed, the crab moved onto its back whenever a magnet was held above its organ of balance.

Cancer and Capricorn

During the winter solstice the sun is in a situation which is in complete conflict with its nature as a source of light. It is in a contradictory position which it begins to resolve by rising. It is precisely this conflict with the environment which Capricorn seeks again and again. Its whole lifestyle consists of a battle against circumstances in order to overcome them. No creature of the zodiac expresses such perseverance against everything around it as strongly as

Capricorn. The cliffs are its home and it remains loyal to these regions even in the coldest winter. Thus nature has given it a position of incredible resistance to the elements unleashed against it. It battles with the downward-pulling forces of the earth and is the greatest victor of them all.

During the summer solstice the sun is in a situation which corresponds entirely with its true nature, and yet it abandons this position. After the summer solstice the sun starts to move back in a crab-like fashion. From that time on, its direction is determined by forces in the earth. Its behaviour is determined by something of a lower order than its own true nature.

The crab expresses this in such a way that the environment becomes more important than its own activities. It avoids conflicts and tension with the surroundings as far as possible, using them to protect itself against the dangers which are lurking there. It hides away in a hole; it incorporates the hard matter of the earth in its armour. It has numerous mechanical pieces of equipment. It never relies on its own agility and strength, as does Capricorn.

A creature such as the mountain goat has to 'improvise' incessantly in order to cope with changing situations. It depends on an extremely varied use of its simple structure.

A crab has tools for every possible situation. It is rather like a walking collection of solutions to every problem which may befall it.

Looking at the great skills of Capricorn from the point of view of the crab, it is clear that there is a great weakness in the fact that Capricorn never seeks protection, and could so easily become extinct. Because of its lifestyle, it is more exposed to danger. Considering the crab from the point of view of Capricorn, we see that all its precautions for survival are at the expense of freedom of movement. The crab has the least freedom of all the creatures of the zodiac.

Aries

By about March 21 the arc of the sun reaches its fastest
daily increase. From then on it is above the horizon for
longer than it is below, and light therefore dominates over
darkness. However, it is not only light which dominates
over darkness, but because the sun's arc increases quickly,
the dark is powerfully rejected every day. During this time,
the emphasis is completely on the sunrise. Every day the
sun succeeds in liberating itself from the earth a little
earlier, and rising a little higher. Every day sunset is
delayed a little longer. Every day a new and powerful
thrust of light seems to batter against the dark. Though
the latter recedes, its strength cannot be mistaken, for
gradually the speed at which the sun's arc grows slows
down. Everything indicates that the light emitted by the
sun during the time of Aries is full of a young, fresh,
vigorous force.

The most noticeable characteristic of rams is the way in
which they fight. They stand at a distance opposite each
other. They seem to agree on the moment when they start
to run, and then crash into each other at full speed with
their heavy horns. Slowly they step back until they reach
a certain distance, and then they start again, galloping
towards each other, resulting in a thundering collision. For
a long time they batter each other with such violence that
any other skull would break into pieces. But the ram will
not cease until it loses consciousness or falls down dead.

One cannot imagine anything more basic and ferocious
than this style of fighting. Each creature seems to count on
the fact that the other one will keep to the rules of the
game and be just as direct as itself.

It is as though I were to say to myself: 'That thing is in
my way, and I do not feel like going around it. Therefore I
will have to batter it aside with all my strength.' If I were
a ram, it would be intolerable to know that another had
just as hard a skull as mine.

In their actions animals make use of a great variety of mechanical principles and material characteristics. In this case the ram's body has a certain degree of density and impenetrability, so that parts can collide. In ancient times this feature of rams was used as a model. In siege warfare the Romans mounted a heavy battering ram on scaffolding with an iron ram's head at the front. It was pushed forward until the ram's head touched the wall. The battering ram was pulled back by a group of soldiers and then let go, ramming the wall with tremendous force. This illustrates a characteristic of solid matter which is not only impenetrable to other matter, but also stops light from passing. An opaque object always constitutes a dark spot. When a hole is made in a wall, it allows light to penetrate though, of course, it would have been intended as a means of conquering the enemy. Hardness not only gives matter its solidity, but can be used to break open the way to light.

Like mountain goats, wild sheep inhabit the mountains on and above the tree line among the bare rocks. Why is it that domesticated sheep have become so docile and defenceless? Have they not retained any of their original nature, like goats have?

Lambs are born in early spring. Initially they are snow-white, bright creatures with flattened faces. The whole fleece is a compact mass of countless curls. This creates a poignant impression of tender innocence and helplessness. They can be playful and dance about. Then they suddenly gambol towards their mother, press their faces into the wool and start sucking, pushing and pulling vigorously. Their little tails wag with pure delight.

As they get older, they become quieter and more tranquil. The sheep is a creature of complete surrender and defencelessness. It can be badly injured and will not defend itself, or even make a noise. It likes to eat well, just like goats do, but is also satisfied with poor food. In addition, its whole body constantly provides us with a valuable material. Few creatures are so productive while grazing on such poor food.

In a flock, sheep behave in a stupid way. They blindly follow behind the creature in front which takes the initiative. A whole flock of sheep can hesitate at a minor obstacle, but if one takes the decisive step, the rest of the flock will follow.

There seems to be little left of the sheep's proud drive for the heights, where their origin lay. Only rams are different. They are prepared to attack and to oppose other creatures and even people. They have an extremely short temper and difficult character, but their behaviour is also relatively simple compared to that of goats.

The sheep's body shows a great contrast between the massive fleece, and the thin head and legs. This contrast is again encountered in the sweet and light lamb which develops into the unbelievable concentration of strength in the ram's head.

The domestic sheep still shows something of its original habitat where the rough hardness of the earth's element is expressed, as well as the intense light of high altitudes. This pure nature of light accompanied by a powerful driving force is what the sheep has taken with it into the depths.

Traditionally a ram is depicted with the head turned back. Again the emphasis is on what lies before and behind, on the world it has left and on the world ahead which it approaches in a powerful way.

Something similar happens when we conceive an important idea. It rises up from a world undefined in our awareness, and then assumes a concrete form. We experience an illumination — an idea is enlightening.

We shall see that the nature of the ram is concerned with the conception and expression of ideas.

Libra

During the period around September 24 the sun descends at its fastest rate. It moves into the realm of gravity faster than at any other time, and darkness gains a victory over light. However, to begin to restore the balance, the rate of the sun's descent slows down. During this time the emphasis is entirely on the sunset. The sun sinks into an abyss of darkness and every day sets a little earlier and rises a little later. The world of darkness takes up more and more time, while the world of light is contracting.

This corresponds to the nature of a pair of scales. When a weight is placed on one side it is pulled down by the force of gravity. However, a counterweight on the other side slows down this movement and then reverses it, first moving faster again, then slowing down until an equilibrium is reached.

Libra is usually depicted as a pair of hanging copper scales. From the arms hang two pans each suspended by three chains. A pointer at the pivot moves from side to side in the vertical plane. When the scales are moved, the whole thing swings in a pendulum-like movement. However, the motion of the balance itself is extremely rigid.

The scales depend completely on a total surrender to gravity, and the movement is also determined solely by gravity and mass. Yet this movement has the same characteristics as the rising and setting of the sun and other heavenly bodies.

It is easier to understand this movement if we compare it with that of a pendulum. When drawn aside and let go, a pendulum swings back with an accelerating movement. When it reaches its lowest point, its point of ultimate rest, it shoots past this at the greatest speed because of its inertia. Then it slows down until it reaches the highest point on the other side, and after an infinitesimal moment of rest, again moves back at an accelerating rate. There is a constant alternation between the moment of rest at the point where the weight is most unstable, and the fastest movement at the place where the balance will be found. In the extreme positions the movement is restarted by gravity. In the central position the movement is maintained by inertia.

In the extreme position, only the earth has an effect through gravity. On the other hand, the inertia which only has an effect at the central position, completely negates the effect of the earth. We can sense that inertia is independent of the earth and related to the stars from the fact that a long pendulum maintains its direction of swing in relation to the stars, while the earth below it rotates in twenty-four hours.

The scales also move similarly: in the most extreme and unstable positions there is an infinitesimal moment of rest, while the fastest movement occurs exactly at the point of ultimate rest. This also applies to the movement of the tides, the lengthening and shortening of days, the rising and setting of the sun in the course of a day, as well as its heightening and lowering in the course of a year. The combined movement of a number of pendulums can even mirror the looping movements which the planets describe in the sky.

Thus both a pair of scales and a pendulum carry cosmic laws into the realm of the earth's gravity. Like the pendulum, the secret of rhythm, the interaction between two opposing worlds, is contained in the movements of a pair of scales. The weights move in such a way that they are sometimes affected by the force of gravity, and sometimes by those of the universe. In the extreme positions only the downward force of gravity has an effect; for the movements in the middle position, only the stars have an effect from all sides.

Aries and Libra

Like the battering ram, scales are associated with the Romans, though for a totally different reason. With the battering ram they attempted to impose their will on their opponents, while scales stood for justice, the weighing up of the conduct of citizens.

Here again we find contrast between opposite signs of the zodiac. A set of scales has one point of suspension and two weights which make a constant vertical swinging movement. In principle a battering ram has two points of suspension but only one weight, which makes horizontal movements.

The essence of the ram lies in a strong concentration on a centre. Scales essentially are sensitive to the weight at their extremity; the emphasis is on the periphery. A fighting ram is an example of a creature that wishes to determine matters around it entirely by itself, and will not take outside influences into account. A pair of scales has no will of its own: its action is determined entirely by whatever is laid on it.

The ram, a creature expressing the most rigid and immovable side of the earth element, is faced with a dead instrument which balances things in a most sensitive way. The instrument is elevated to something which is otherwise achieved only by living creatures: it is self-regulating and reflects a cosmic context. The animal uses crudely mechanical forces; the mechanism becomes an almost organic creature.

In sheep we are concerned above all with what moves from the inside out; growing a fleece, butting. Sheep do not take into account the existence of the opposite direction. This is also the reason why a sheep does not react. A reaction always depends on taking the environment into account.

Scales are concerned with something which is wholly determined from the outside. This also explains why no

living creature could form this sign of the zodiac, for a
living creature in principle develops from the inside outwards. Only an instrument is constructed from the outside.

The Golden Fleece or other traditions show the ram in
relation to the sun and to gold, and therefore to the world
of daylight. The scales could be depicted surrounded by
stars, by darkness. The figure of Justice holding the scales
is blindfolded, cut off from the light.

Our observations of the different creatures of the zodiac
are an important exercise. Just as each creature shows a
particular tendency, so everyone tends to adopt a one-sided
view and make judgments on this basis. This is one of the
main causes of the lack of understanding between people.
Nothing helps this understanding better than adopting
another person's position to try and consider the world
from that point of view. This aspect was the starting point
for this book.

5. The Zodiac as the Background to Human Life

On 'the four creatures' and man as a synthesis of the animal kingdom

Until now we have referred only to the human element where it was specifically contained within the sign of the zodiac. We will now interpret the signs of nature in such a way that they give us an insight into the nature and mood of man. But just before this we will do the converse — through an insight into the human spirit, we can discover secrets on which the whole structure of nature is based.

Among the symbols which expressed the deepest knowledge of man, is a winged creature comprised of four forms: a bull, a lion, an eagle and an angelic human figure. This symbol is also found in the Bible, both in the Old Testament as Ezekiel's vision which Raphael depicted in his famous painting, as well as in the Revelation to St John where these four creatures bear the throne. Traditionally, as seen in early paintings, these four represent the four writers of the gospels: John as the eagle, Mark as the lion, Luke as the bull, and Matthew as man.

We immediately recognize them as the signs of the zodiac of Taurus, Leo, Scorpio and Aquarius. Each of these signs is connected with the middle of a season. This indicates that ancients saw four cardinal points in the structure of the world. While the principle is in fact supernatural — as indicated by the wings of the four creatures — it forms a hidden structure to the world which is manifested physically as the four separate creatures of the eagle, lion, bull and man.

We can appreciate this ancient symbolism with the help

of the concepts of one of the central discoveries of Rudolf Steiner: the threefold structure of the human organism. He first described this in 1917 in *Riddles of the Soul*. Our soul has three distinct functions: thought, feeling and the will. Each of these functions has a different physical basis.

Thought is of course related to the nervous system, and in particular the brain. However, the seats of the will and of feeling are not located in the brain. The images related to feeling and the will must be clearly distinguished from feeling and the will as such.

Feeling is related to those processes in our body which have a rhythmic pattern, and in particular with heartbeat and respiration. This can easily be seen when observing, for instance the change in heartbeat and breath when frightened, excited or upset. Language reveals many expressions of this as well: for example, the heart is often mentioned in connection with love and hate, courage and fear.

The will is linked to the metabolism and therefore specifically with the processes which take place in the stomach, the blood and the muscles. This is perhaps not so easy to recognize, apart from the obvious fact that we need our muscles for all our actions, and that this involves metabolic processes.

— The centre of the nervous system is located in the head.
— The centre of the rhythmic system is located in the chest.
— The centre of digestion is located in the lower abdomen.

Let us now turn back to the four cosmic creatures.

In cattle the metabolism is enormously developed, while the nervous system is relatively weak in comparison. A large part of their life is devoted to eating and digestion. They achieve tremendous feats of metabolism, eating huge quantities of food which our organs would find completely indigestible.

In the eagle the nervous system is unusually prominent, particularly the eyes, but the sense of balance and muscular reflexes are also highly developed, as is evident from the way in which the bird flies and glides. In comparison, the digestive processes are relatively underdeveloped.

Rudolf Steiner pointed out that the digestive system and the sensory system are constantly vying for supremacy in our constitution. The rhythmic system, particularly the heart, serves to preserve a balance in this. For the lion this balance is the main element in the life processes. Passions often flare up in this creature, releasing tremendous power, and yet he also remains calm and in control. This indicates that the equilibrium achieved is such that the balanced interaction between the muscles and the senses is never disturbed, as it can be, for instance, in a furious bull. Language again points to a strong link between the lion and the heart. When we say that someone has a 'lion's heart,' we mean that they are strong and powerful. We merely have to hear the lion's roar, overpowering the voices of all the other creatures, to know that there is great strength in his voice.

The three parts of the body relate to the world differently. Our head keeps its distance from things. Moving through the world it remains aloof. By contrast our contact with the world is through our limbs, particularly our legs. It is always the chest that assumes a central position.

In this way we see how the head reflects the tendency of the eagle. In the same way, the lower abdomen bears a similarity to the cow, and the chest and arms are reminiscent of the lion.

Furthermore, the eagle reveals some of the aspects of the head: aloof and observing from a distance: the cow is completely dominated by metabolic processes which take place above all in the lower body, and the tendency of its legs to push and thrust even reaches its head. The lion is largely governed by the rhythmic processes which are concentrated in the chest, and it has a basic capacity (which is refined in human hands) for grasping things. What is expressed on a large scale — though in a very one-sided way — in animals, is synthesized in man's organization in a harmonious and reserved way.

These observations help to understand the link between the development of consciousness and the working of life processes which we will be referring to repeatedly below.

Observing humans throughout the course of their life, we first see tiny creatures who sleep for most of the day and have little consciousness of themselves or their surroundings even during their waking hours. The need for sleep gradually decreases with age, and at the same time consciousness increases. However, it is during the early unconscious stages that the body's growth and metabolic processes take place in the strongest form. Gradually the capacity for growth decreases and even the capacity for regeneration becomes weaker. When we observe the adult we find that the life processes have been preserved most strongly in the lower abdomen. The metabolic processes in the brain are weak and the capacity for regeneration is almost entirely absent. Yet it is exactly at the spot where life is ebbing fastest that consciousness develops. Conversely we are barely aware of the lower abdomen where the life processes are still powerful.

Comparing the eagle to the cow, the former is much more awake. The eagle operates strongly in the activity of the most conscious sensory organ — the eye. In the cow, one of the less acute senses, the sense of smell, is predominant. However, the creature which is the more awake lives amongst the processes of death, while the cow lives amongst the flourishing life processes. Again the lion assumes an intermediary position.

It is superficial to say that nature wakes up in the spring and falls asleep again in the autumn. Rudolf Steiner emphasized a more profound point of view, which sheds light on one of the most important links between man and nature. The dying away which takes place in the autumn can be compared to what takes place in our head in the daytime to allow consciousness. The great growth processes in spring can be compared with the unconscious life processes in our lower abdomen, and with the regenerative processes which work during our sleep. The signs of the zodiac represent the same processes where the bull is the sign of spring and the scorpion (the eagle), the sign of autumn.

When we wake up, we become wintry; when we are asleep, summer is within us. This is how we can think of the awakening of the earth organism as winter approaches and its sleep when summer comes.

The relationship between death and consciousness, or rather, between restrained life processes and consciousness, was probably expressed for the first time in modern terms by Rudolf Steiner. And yet this relation is quite obvious when we study nature and human life.

One of the most tragic aspects of our culture, is the frantic and one-sided aim of maintaining of life forces, the search for eternal youth. This can only be at the expense of full human development, which can only take place with the highest consciousness. On the other hand, we see the most violent destructive processes taking place in our society through a disregard of consequences, or simply a lack of awareness. This points to the law: forces which are not understood, that is, not penetrated by full consciousness become uncontrollable and destructive.

In the signs of the zodiac the scorpion symbolizes some of the dangers which are contained in death processes which are not understood.

However, the eagle indicates a direction for using these forces of death in a beneficial way. It is only by raising our consciousness to the highest spiritual life and by means of an immeasurable drive to raise ourselves above the bondage of material processes that we can ennoble the forces of death. Left to themselves they have no purpose, and always go too far. Our noble task is to use the possibilities available and to unravel the true meaning, even of death.

In the past people learned much more pictorially. Aspects of threefold nature that we try to understand as abstract concepts were once illustrated in great images. If we learn to understand the language of living images, as well as that of abstract concepts, endless possibilities are opened up to us. New relationships are continually revealed the more we study these images.

The images discussed above indicate that man, who initially seemed to be a self-contained and complete creature, actually has links through the three systems of organs with areas of nature: a high area, a central area and a deep area. Thus there is also a threefold order to be found in nature. To understand this more clearly we can use the human organization as a key, while the images for understanding the threefold structure of man can again be taken from nature.

We can only learn to understand the meaning of the signs of the zodiac when we realize that the above not only applies in relation to the three animals, but that there is a corresponding relationship between all the animals and man.

The immense variety and one-sidedness which occurs in nature is synthesized in the structure of man.

Lorenz Oken and Goethe first introduced this idea: man is a synthesis of the animal kingdom and the animal kingdom is composed of elements of man.

Other realms of nature are similar; for instance, there is a close relationship between man and the plant world as well as between man and the mineral world. Man is a microcosm. The wholeness of the macrocosm is expressed in the signs of the zodiac, and it is possible to recognize all aspects of man there, when we have learned to understand this imagery.

Introduction to the twelve characters

The signs of the zodiac as a whole describe the whole range of forces which operates both in nature and in man. Every image individually refers to a single effect with a particular, clearly defined quality. When someone's nature is strongly dominated by a one-sidedness, their whole being and behaviour have a particular stamp, and they become a particular type of person. A study of human nature shows that there are twelve such types.

We have so far discussed mainly the one-sided effects which occur in relation to the signs of the zodiac, but we will now turn to the twelve human characters.

Astrology has taught us a great deal about such characters which is mainly empirical knowledge based on rich traditions. However, we will not refer to the typical astrological traditions or to the results of astrology. The ancient traditions will virtually only be used in so far as they provide us with the images.

The characters we describe are methodologically derived from the Rudolf Steiner's anthroposophical view of man. We characterize the forces or complexes of forces which operate in human lives by asking what sort of person would be the result if the influence of a particular image were totally dominant. As in reality the influences can never be so one-sided, these characters could not really exist, but they help to typify the tendency. It is only in the field of art that we sometimes come across very pure characters.

We will endeavour to follow a path which is easily accessible to our understanding, for we should avoid matters that we do not understand. However, these relationships cannot only be explained and understood in terms of everyday logic.

We are pioneering a way here where no clear path exists. Rudolf Steiner has left us a number of clues to follow, as well as some tremendous insights. To find the way certain skills are needed, as well as a great deal of perseverance.

There are some dangers. One is that of superficiality. Another is that of a one-sided interest. It is tempting to turn straight to one's own reflection, but this is particularly pointless. One can find out what sort of a person one is in ordinary life, but in order to understand why one is a particular way, and what this means in terms of responsibilities, one needs to study all the signs of the zodiac.

One of the greatest dangers is that the acquired insights

are misused. We hope that an attempt to shed some light in this field will have a beneficial effect.

As well as examples from art, a number of relevant characters from literature are typical of particular signs of the zodiac. In many cases the study serves to give a more defined and detailed character. Sometimes we also pass from literature to the imagery contained in myths, which can shed a great deal of light.

The Taurus and Scorpio characters

In everyone's life there are certain situations which involve coping with difficult tasks, and we will take two examples to illustrate this. When preparing for an examination two very different attitudes can be adopted. One is to approach the task directly and unconditionally, set to work on it, and complete the whole job without thinking of how it would be possible to save time and energy. The contents of all the books are simply patiently absorbed. It's like taking up a spade, digging the earth where it has to be removed, taking it in a wheelbarrow to the place where it has to be dumped, and persevering at all costs until the job is done. Another attitude is to start by taking a careful look at the job in hand and giving it some thought. In other words, one starts by viewing it from a distance to gain an overall picture and tries to find out whether there might be ways of saving energy, achieving better results and completing the task more quickly. Perhaps it is possible to draw up a better schedule of work or find better tools; perhaps natural forces could be used in the form of horsepower or a steam engine; one could even try to pass the work on so that other people completed the task.

The strange thing is that what in one person may only be the slightest tendency can dominate the whole life of another. If we look carefully, we can always find something in ourselves that corresponds to even the most extreme attitudes. Everyone possesses a complete range of traits, though some in a very unobtrusive form. We can empathize with another by exaggerating particular characteristics in the imagination.

There are people who immediately set to work with all their strength at every task that comes their way and try to complete it, nose to the grindstone and plodding all the way. They do not really trust their own power for thought, and may perhaps be rather dull or unintelligent, but they certainly have lots of vitality. They only feel really happy when they have a heavy task at hand, for they long to be really tired. The more they come up against obstacles and exhaust themselves, the more they feel liberated from the dulling influence of their excessive vitality. They are even grateful to accept a certain degree of pain. They only feel comfortable when some of their excessive health is taken away. Such people have a constitution reminiscent of bull-like *Taurus*. The metabolic system is predominant, while the nervous system functions comparatively sluggishly. The design of the body as a whole is determined originally by the nervous system. In this type of person with a relatively weak nervous system, the structure of the body is generally rather ungainly and undifferentiated. The shape of the body tends to be rather full, the figure may be stocky, very broad and squarish, possibly even with a bull neck, that is, a short, broad neck. This means that the separation between the head and the body is so slight that the blood can rise rather too easily, so that conditions which should be limited to the body rise up to the head. The limbs may in extreme cases also be short and stocky. It is quite possible for someone to have marked Taurean characteristics without having a stocky build. It is also quite possible for Taureans such as this to be intelligent, to learn easily and understand the relationships between things when they are explained to them. However, they will still find it difficult to acquire insights independently, for in the cognitive field all subject matter must always be thoroughly taken in and digested. They will have most difficulty with regard to developing original and productive ideas. They are rarely inspired and therefore find it difficult to determine a direction for themselves.

Because of this mentality, Taureans tends to be dependent on something outside themselves. The whole course of their life may be determined by traditional ideas and arrangements, and they will be scrupulous about passing these traditions on. However, they may also develop a tendency to serve others wholeheartedly. In general they will attempt to assume a subservient role, and therefore to hold others in greater esteem. It is clear that this tendency could easily lead to a state of complete dependence. However, it happens all too often that noble Taureans allow themselves to be used for nefarious purposes by a less worthy person because they lacks the capacity to see through things. Thus although this is a serious weakness, their great strength lies in the capacity to dedicate themselves completely to the task of helping someone else to realize their ideas, or to realize the ideas which they have received from someone else. As long as they are quite clear about what they are doing, they will work like no other, and in this way achieve the greatest things.

Emotionally their nature may be easy-going and even good-hearted. They do not begrudge anyone anything, for they tend to suffer more from a surfeit than a lack of things themselves.

However, it should not be forgotten that there is a great deal of tension caused by their excessive will. Usually they will be fairly peaceful and tolerant of the environment. However, some things will let loose the full force of their passions. When this happens, they lose all power of reason, and in this condition, can cause the most dreadful accidents.

The *Scorpio* character reveals the second attitude to life described above. Figuratively speaking, this type have a strong antipathy to getting their hands dirty or to exerting themselves physically. They are over-intelligent and their brain functions virtually automatically. They constantly try to think of ways in which they can achieve what they want without making an effort. They behave like a head in search of limbs. In general, mental activity is developed at the expense of vital life forces to such an extent (see page 80) that they might be seriously damaged. This may express itself in terms of physical weakness, but even if the constitution is not significantly affected, this character will still feel impaired in some way. They suffer from an inner lack and are therefore prone to feel badly done by.

Because of this there is often a lack of moral understanding — a lack of constraint. In extreme cases an understanding of morality may be absent to such a degree that the person concerned could be said to be morally blind. How can this be explained?

The natural world is permeated with infinite wisdom and harmony. The structure of our bodies, and therefore our related system of mobility, corresponds in every way with the effect of gravity and all the mechanical laws; our respiratory organs are tuned in to the composition of the air and function in harmony with cosmic rhythms; our digestive organs are able to digest vegetable and animal substances in order to maintain our life processes. However, there are also processes which constantly disturb this harmony, in particular, the functioning of our waking consciousness. The fact that this causes problems for our constitution is revealed by the need for regular periods of sleep. When we wake up, we step out of the area of deep cosmic healing and harmony. Morality is based on the search for inner harmony, and maintaining the correct relation with the environment. True morality contains a reflection of a divine cosmic order. Thus morality must be founded on a healthy interplay of life forces. At least a small degree of observation of the way in which our character fits into the cosmic order is necessary if we are to find a basis for our morality. The Scorpio character is too much awake because they separate themselves from a healthy relationship with the world more than any other character. In contrast, the Taureans' behaviour shows that they likes to feel part of the whole. They never feel happier than when they are a single cog among all the other cogs in the great machinery of life.

While the Scorpio type distance themselves from the deeper relation with the cosmic order, they retain the urge to assume a position of leadership and wisdom. They do not feel that others are equal to them and have no need to take them into account. To them they are objects which need to be led. In fact, they delight in leading them on the basis of a knowledge of their own deeper laws. In extreme cases they will even try to separate other beings and natural forces from their cosmic context in order to substitute their own influence completely.

Let us return to our starting point, to see how this single-minded attitude can deteriorate into complete immorality.

It begins fairly innocently: how can they achieve as much as possible with as little effort as possible? Starting to use things to their advantage, they are all too ready to be helped by others. It is necessary to distinguish what aspects of things and people are useful, objects are so appraised in a clever way to achieve a particular goal. At the next stage they are only interested in the usefulness of everything they encounter. Anything that cannot be used is simply discarded. It no longer matters whether another person might be capable of other achievements or might have a will of their own, or whether they suffer intolerably in performing their duties. The leader's own desires unconditionally take priority over the suffering of others.

In the final stage which is deep in moral darkness, the Scorpio type is not merely undisturbed by the suffering of others, but actually start to enjoy the suffering they inflict. This trait is found in the scheming nature of people who enjoy undermining the interaction between people or groups by means of small but carefully planned intrigues, in such a way that people turn against each other, or even injure or destroy each other.

These activities may develop to a barely imaginable degree. An extreme Scorpio character is possessed by a sort of envy of others whose health is strong or who possess inner greatness. They will never risk an honest, open trial of strength, but enjoy the weaknesses and vulnerable spots of others, and use these to bring them down or even destroy them. They will not rest before they have created a situation in which they can once again feel superior.

In Felix Dahn's book *Ein Kampf um Rom* the character who portrays the strongest Scorpio traits is Theodora, the Empress of the East Roman Empire. By means of all sorts of intrigues in which she stops at nothing, she attempts to influence the events around her at court and in the whole Empire. Her friend is Antonina, the wife of one of the great generals, Belisar. This woman is dependent on her husband in a rather simple way, and is remarkable for her flourishing health. The former trait arouses Theodora's contempt, the second a terrible envy. So she tries to destroy her friend.

This clear description of the Scorpio and Taurus characters can also be found in Shakespeare's *Othello*. This time it is Iago who destroys Othello, a characteristic Taurean, in the typical Scorpio way. He achieves this by a complicated intrigue, totally 'poisoning' Othello's personality with suspicion and jealousy. In his whipped-up rage, Othello murders his beloved wife. This is a very pure example of a strong will, full of passion and emotion, which is too open to the influence and suggestions of another. And Iago, excessively cunning, attempts to destroy Othello's common sense completely. He substitutes his own version.

When acting in a conscious way, we are led by the head. It attempts to keep a distance from the dynamic interplay of forces. It is faced by something more powerful than itself, and constantly has to tame it and keep it at bay. In contrast, our metabolic system is concerned mainly with the other functions which it supports. It is completely geared to serving. It is prepared to surrender wholly to everything emanating from the head.

We see the behaviour of the Taurus and Scorpio characters reflected in a person's constitution. When Scorpions try to control forces without this being noticeable externally, and attempt to reduce or destroy something great and powerful, they do the same as our head does to the rest of our body when we are awake. If Taureans wish to support and elevate another, and when they constantly make all their strength available to increase and reinforce another's power, they are simply doing what our own metabolic system does for our head.

In the true *eagle* character a very different aspect of thinking from that of the Scorpio character is apparent. If it is possible to raise our thoughts to the fundamental nature of all being, the relationships between everything around us become manifest. From this point of view we learn to understand the position of all creatures and things in the divine creative plan, and the way in which things influence and determine each other. Everything becomes part of the tremendous pattern and interplay of forces. If we observe only what can be perceived through the senses, the environment appears as a collection of separate objects, but if we rise above this in our thoughts, the separate details recede and are assimilated in the net of relationships to form a tremendous cosmic tableau.

People with the true eagle nature have adopted this as a lifestyle. They always develop a superior attitude towards the ordinary things of life. Each particular object and situation is seen in the largest context, so that the eagle character is barely affected by it, and initially does not experience its important influence. To anyone else, this may easily create an impression of a cool, pride. They live as though everything that is happening in the world is always in their consciousness, and even as though they can oversee the whole of the past, present and future. Their feeling and will only fully develop when they rise to the greatest heights of philosophy. They only really come to life in this element and become glowingly passionate about it. They are only satisfied with the greatest perspectives.

However, it is precisely this trait which can chill the atmosphere around them when the small things of daily life require attention. Because their elevated thoughts develop at the expense of vital life forces, they live in an atmosphere which may be elevated, but is also rather dead. In particular, they understand the world as it has developed, and in so far as they can foresee the future, they see the required developments resulting from the past.

From their height it is not easy to grasp the individual. Of course, they will be quick to understand why someone responds or acts in a particular way, but they are generally too inclined to see every event as an example of a general pattern. When their life element consists of the generally applicable, how can they appreciate the absolutely irreplaceable particular element of every individual, not to mention the uniqueness of every sensory impression? It is precisely these special details relating to man and nature that contain the seed of life for the new future. From the height at which the eagle character views the world below, everything seems rather undifferentiated. Above all, it is very difficult to distinguish between high and low, and give more weight to one or another matter. They tend to underestimate the significance of individual things or creatures. In fact, everything the eagle sees, and everything the eagle character sees, is rather flat, painted against the earth. There is a very real risk that they will ignore others, or even despise them. Problems arise for them when thoughts have to be translated into actions. The whole will is aimed at gliding above ordinary events, and now they have to change direction and seek out the depths. It is symbolic of the flying eagle: the tremendous plane taken up by the wingspan and the huge encompassing movement of the beating of the wings. And yet the legs which serve to establish a link with the earth are withered and underdeveloped. When this bird swoops down into the depths, it pounces on its prey and immediately tears it from the ground to carry it up back into the heights.

In the same way a human eagle character cannot easily

urge others on to strong deeds. However, if people have a drive to act, the eagle character will give them the possibility to carry this out in the highest sense and in harmony with the cosmic order.

The eagle's eye is small, but wide open, with a strong, sharp gaze aimed at the distance. The area around the eye is rigid and hard. This characteristic is also found in human eagle characters, who do not show their emotions in their gaze. When impressions impinge upon them, they repress their emotions and observe them from a distance, like a tableau. Passionate hot-blooded responses do not arise in them. By contrast, Taureans are unable to keep impressions at a distance. Everything they observe immediately enters their 'flesh and blood.' As a result, they constantly tend to exaggerate every single thing or person, and see it as the whole world. They are unable to keep things at a distance and remain objective. On the other hand, the eagle character increases the distance to such an extent that individual things are seen too small.

In *Ein Kampf um Rom* there is also a figure with characteristic eagle traits, combined with some of the characteristics of Scorpio. This is Narses, the greatest general of the Byzantine Empire. He is described as a crippled and delicate figure, very small in stature. Nevertheless, he makes a deep impression on his surroundings, partly because of his penetrating eagle's gaze. He is as a great a politician as a general, setting everything in motion and arranging matters with the power of thought. He never enters the battle, as he is physically unable to, but follows the army on a litter. He employs the savage fighting spirit of certain tribes in his plans, and ultimately attempts to destroy Germanic tribes with other Germanic tribes. Finally, he succeeds in virtually eradicating the Goths and removing this threat to Byzantium. However, he does not do this out of hatred or ambition, but in order to fulfil a profound historical destiny which he understands.

He is capable of rising above everything to such an

extent that he even exposes Theodora's intrigues and thus destroys her.

Looking at these characteristics, the greatest conflict seems to be between the eagle and scorpion characters. The former draws everything up into an objective cosmic context, while the latter constantly threatens to draw everything down to satisfy his own desires.

However, there are also characteristics which these two have in common. They both work with the forces of death with a skill that no other type possesses. Both are so obsessed with the ideas in their own mind that they are hardly open to any outside influences. Because of this, they are rarely able to surrender to another being or impression.

In this respect they are in complete contrast with the nature of the Taurus character. Possibly the greatest virtue of that character, the will to serve others, is almost totally lacking in them. The eagle and scorpion characters are certain of their own tasks and do not feel the weight of the task of another.

Leo and Aquarius characters

During the course of life one is sometimes surrounded by many people, and then withdraws back into loneliness. When one is alone, there may be times when the very silence seems to have a voice. The most delicate and tender aspect of the hidden essence of things can reveal itself to us. It is particularly when one has spent a long time of great activity and then withdraws, feeling an image of the deeper, true self welling up from the depths, that one becomes aware of something more profound and encompassing in oneself than the restricted and one-sided being which we are when we exist surrounded by activity.

However, there is also a great delight in living on the crest of the wave of outer life. Then we can test our strength, we can experience everything, even the most shaking events, still being able to cope with every situation. This means that the inner balance is continually disrupted and there is a constant struggle to restore it.

Some people have a permanent tendency to the former condition. They soon tire of external life and feel damaged and brought down by it. They seek a cure by turning inwards. For them the true source of their humanity is surrounded by an area of great silence and solitude.

For others this attitude is completely alien to their nature. They focus all their attention on the world and feel themselves to be in a constant struggle to maintain their inner peace, even in the most turbulent situations.

The latter, represented as the *Leo* character, live on everything that is experienced through the senses, and react to this with their strong heartbeat and the rhythm of their breathing. This does not mean that they are necessarily good at observation or observe things very deeply. Everything which enters us from the environment is a sort of attack on our organism. The Leo character experiences sense impressions as something which gives rise to passions and emotions. Why does this tendency prevail?

We have previously seen that our structure is composed in accordance with the principle of polarity. There is a great tension between the sensory-nervous system and the metabolic-limb system. This tension achieves a balance through the rhythmic system. In the Leo character a great deal of attention seems to be focused on this rhythmic system. In creating the organism the spiritual essence was deeply involved with this area, resulting in great power in this respect. Having this power means that there is also a drive to use it. Thus Leo characters are not only oriented towards the sensory world, but often seek a very lively environment to find an outlet for their strength. They feel comfortable in their body, for what comfort is greater than that of the peace, when trials and tribulations have been overcome? Their sense of comfort becomes true happiness when their inner balance is put to a severe test and they still succeed in overcoming the situation. As a rule Leo characters will collect people around them and test their strength against them. They are a born leaders. In some senses they are completely externalised, aimed at the outside world. Yet there is a lofty aspect to them which is often expressed in a regal bearing. Because of the rhythmic organization a close link is maintained with cosmic rhythms. A restoring and healing strength emanates from it. Leo characters bear a profound and healthy imprint of the cosmos within themselves. They can afford to establish far-reaching links with the earth, for the celestial world will not let them go.

These sort of people can never really be unbalanced. They can become furious when irritated, but will never do anything reckless in a violent fury, as the Taurean character can. They may strike out with strength and accuracy, but will never surrender themselves to their anger. Whatever happens, they will immediately use it to improve their position, and afterwards will soon forget the incident. Their whole behaviour is rather like this. They do not have to think very hard about what to do. Observations can immediately be followed by action — and this will often have an effect which others are unable to achieve even after the most careful and lengthy consideration. They are not concerned so much about achieving ambitious goals, such as those of the Sagittarius character, but rather with mastering circumstances and establishing an order under their control.

One can be a Leo in very different fields of life. An obvious field is that of politics and statesmanship. Leos in the scientific field will not rest before they have totally mastered their subject matter. This can soon result in a position of recognition. But there is no great drive to develop new ideas or to establish a profound new system.

Leos accepts the world as it is, as long as they can be central in it.

The above description shows that thought processes do not play a very great role in the Leo character. They may assimilate many scientific ideas, but they will never make much distinction between facts and laws, and will assimilate them in much the same way. Everything is absorbed into memory as useful material without making an effort to follow all the thought processes laboriously.

The wise leading principle is completely central in their feelings. Feelings give them a sense of certainty in every situation and are the real drive behind their actions.

Thus, thinking and will in the Leo character are both closely related to, and governed by feeling. Leos owe their inexhaustible energy and certainty to this. What about feeling itself? This has a liberal quality. As long as Leo characters are recognized for what they are, and allowed to go their own way, they will not be affected by trivialities and will not obstruct other people, even when they are rather unpleasant. They have little time for minor antipathies. However, if anyone really gets in their way, he must watch out for the terrible reaction that threatens to engulf him. It is also difficult to evoke any great sympathy in them. Their positive feelings are also liberal. One does not feel that one is easily recognized, because they tend to overlook many things, but once we have earned their respect, they have ample attention for us. They are generous and understand the art of showing their appreciation.

If we consider the world as it appears through our senses as a complete reality, we see a wealth of individual and wholly unrelated details. The animal kingdom is not even perceived in terms of different species, but only as countless individual creatures, some of which resemble others. It is only possible to classify these creatures, in terms of species, families, orders and so on, through the thought processes. Our mind is always looking for unity in the complexity of the world, and will succeed in finding it. However, the mind does not discover this unity in the outside world, but in the inner self. And yet, if the thinking is thorough, the unity that is discovered turns out to be related to the very diversity which confronts us. In this way, one approaches the world from two sides, through the senses and through the spirit. To the senses the world appears as diverse individual phenomena; for the spirit everything flows together to form a unity. We have seen how the lion is open to the outside world and tries to assimilate and control the diversity in its powerful grasp. *Aquarius* stands before an inner threshold, so that he is able to enter the area of the all-encompassing unity. Leo is concerned with external phenomena, with the appearance of things and beings, while Aquarius seeks the entrance to the area where their essence is protected. As long as one is merely thinking, one remains before the threshold. However, it is possible to enter into the area beyond by developing a new sort of perception, an inner observation. In anthroposophy Rudolf Steiner has shown the different animal species to be spiritual beings. The spiritual being of each species is comparable to the spiritual being of each person. They are full of a powerful wisdom, but they do not know love. They act entirely in accordance with great cosmic harmony and obey the wisdom permeating the whole world. We humans, on the other hand, can merely arrive laboriously at a wise way of behaving, if the strength of our love is great enough to form a profound link with the world.

Aquarius characters are most at home in the spiritual area. Here they can move with the same ease as Leo does in the outside world. However, they may all too readily be stopped at the threshold, with only a vague sense and idea of everything which lies beyond. Even if this is the case, the threshold could become a source of important insights, forces and strengths to them.

Aquarius characters reveal a deep mystery. It is no coincidence that of all the creatures living on the earth only man is able to reveal the unity referred to above. For as we have seen, the body of man is merely a great reflection of everything else in the world. He himself is the living image of the spiritual unity which he sees in his inner self. Thus, what we observe is at the same time the complex of creative forces which compose his constitution, and the complex of forces on which the diversity of creation is based.

True Aquarius characters are predestined to base their life on an inner communion with the spirit. However, these days they will find it very difficult to find their way. They will rarely find the entrance to those places where they can assimilate a philosophy to suit them. They will have even greater difficulty in finding a place where their abilities truly come into their own. Therefore they will tend to become reclusive, and to flee the ordinary society of people.

Just as they withdraw easily from society into their own lifestyle, their spiritual essence strongly rejects the connection with their physical body. Leo characters, on the other hand, are fully ready to assimilate the physical aspect. They dive deeply into the world where diversity abounds, and are disposed to fall into a strongly one-sided nature. This type of person has gone a long way towards becoming an animal, for one of the first characteristics of animals is their one-sided nature.

Aquarius characters are people with an unusually strong connection to the archetypal image of man. In this respect, every form of specialization is foreign to them; none of the three forces of the soul is clearly dominant, and as a result, their whole nature may have a rather indeterminate character. As a rule, his physical strength is not very great. The Leo character has strength enough to dominate the world as it is; the Aquarius character still has a lot of unused creative force.

How will the fully developed Aquarius character use this force? When they encounter a phenomenon which interests them, they tend to contemplate it patiently or meditate on it until they finally discover how it springs from the great cosmic unity and how they should relate to it. Thus if they become interested in another person, they will see all sorts of disharmony. Such disharmony is founded on a distorted or damaged relationship with the spiritual world. In a sense they are predisposed to understand this, and are therefore able to give advice and even suggest remedies.

For them it is clear that there is a healing plant for every complaint. While every plant is basically healthy it is nevertheless a deviation, or one-sided aspect of the archetypal, ideal plant. Similarly, every complaint is a sort of deviation from the archetypal human essence. One deviation can be used to remove another.

The greatest skills of Aquarians lie in their capacity to help their fellow humans to find the correct relationship with their inner origins. They can show them the way towards true humanity. The strength which they use goes beyond pity. It could even be called a shared will. The word 'pity' suggests shared suffering, but we are concerned here with the shared will to help another being fulfil the deepest meaning of the existence.

The whole nature of the Aquarius character means that everything related to it is difficult to approach. They cannot be characterized as easily as some. Moreover, impressions of this nature are elusive, and disappear easily. Therefore different methods must be employed to approach it.

In the polarity of Leo and Aquarius we are concerned with the contrast between man and animal. Rudolf Steiner pointed out the great difference in the experience of pain felt by humans and animals. In a sense, pain is much worse for an animal than it is for a human being, as an animal is wholly a creature of the soul, completely taken over by its perceptions. An animal in pain *is* pain. It surrenders unconditionally to the pain. Human beings who also have a self and are spiritual beings, can raise themselves above pain. They can even reap a great harvest for their development from their suffering. Rudolf Steiner's described this: 'Wisdom is crystallized pain.' For humans there is a point to suffering. It is a deeply tragic fact of the life of an animal that suffering has no reward. The Leo character is characterized by a pleasure drive, a life of well-being and even an avoidance of suffering. The Aquarius character is the opposite. Aquarians avoid the pleasures of life outside themselves and have a tendency towards asceticism. Their nature, more than that of any other, is prepared to fully confront suffering and not to rest until it has bestowed upon them the crown of wisdom.

An animal does not know what it is to give and to receive. Of course, it takes what it needs and what pleases it, but it does not receive anything from another creature as an expression of this, and it does not tolerate anything for the sake of another being. A true human being accepts others as they are, and is able to incorporate all expressions of this with equanimity. Furthermore, they are able to give another being something purely because it is good for that person, even if it is at their own expense. They are familiar with something which we could call the reverse of desire — joy in the satisfaction and well-being of another person. The Aquarius character is always concerned with the interaction with the deepest aspect of other beings.

The nature of the Leo character is much simpler. For example, if Leos wish to establish order in occupied territory, or even in a whole nation, they will simply suppress any sign of opposition or revolt. They consider inner feelings quite unimportant.

In the nature of both the Leo and Aquarius type there is a drive to rise above lower considerations. The Leo character does this by suppressing these lower considerations, basing his position on this. The Aquarius character throws off the lower considerations and turns directly towards higher ones.

To provide some clearer outlines we will summarize some of the Aquarius characteristics. Their thinking has a contemplative, meditative character. It is not very dependent on logic, for that is mainly a technique, and they seek a direct way into inner reality. They attempt to develop every serious thought until it becomes transparent. To them the thought itself only has a value as a sort of outpost, as an organ of perception for spiritual reality. Their feelings attain great depth. They are prepared to experience anything. They try not to drown in pleasure and not to avoid suffering, so that they develop a power of perception through the feelings. As they have a tendency to want to understand everything and to consider everything they encounter in great depth, they do not develop strong personal sympathies or antipathies. Their will provides little contact with the world outside themselves. Thus they will not find it easy to establish a position. Everything in them is aimed at helping, curing and serving others. However, this service is based on their own insight, and as a rule that will be much greater than that of the person they are helping. It could be described as a sort of royal service, for the question which inspires them is how they can help others to achieve their true humanity.

There is a very striking passage in Schiller's *Don Carlos* in which King Philip II and Marquis Posa have a serious discussion. This discussion seems strongly influenced by the aspects of Leo and Aquarius. This does not mean that Philip acts entirely as a Leo character and Posa as the Aquarius character. Posa defends the rights of the free man, which are completely suppressed by the king's tyrannical government. His famous line, 'I cannot serve a tyrant,' is spoken in this context. He rejects all external functions. He dares to express all his ideals because that which he sees in the spirit is more important for him than the king's mercy, or even his own life. He also pleads for freedom of thought. He succeeds in touching upon such deeply hidden chords that these almost succeed in elevating the hardened king to a more noble humanity. The king clearly reveals some of the dubious aspects of the Leo nature. He demands of his subjects that they honour him slavishly, and will not tolerate any who might rise on their own merits.

Another example of a relationship between two people which seems to have strong connections with the aspects of Aquarius and Leo can be found in C.F. Meyer's *Der Heilige*. The king is a raw force of nature, a fighter who takes what he likes with complete lack of concern, even when this is at the expense of others. In contrast, his chancellor is a highly cultivated man who has not developed a great deal of strength outwardly, but nevertheless dominates the whole environment because of his unusually great spirit. At first, he lives in the atmosphere of Leo, even in great splendour. He is following the fashion. Nevertheless, in the background there is a spot to which he can retreat, a sort of fairy-tale castle for his daughter, whom he guards jealously.

Later, when he becomes archbishop, he adopts a totally ascetic lifestyle, and without taking any overt action, develops such an influence that it affects the king's life and plans. At one point the king is actually totally taken over by the atmosphere created by the archbishop when he lashes himself to his grave.

In *Ein Kampf um Rom* the aspects of Leo and Aquarius are depicted in Theoderik and his minister Cassiodorus. Theoderik appears as a universal figure which could hardly be identified with any image, though constant references are made to the lion and the eagle. He has certainly developed enormous dominant strength which he uses to hold sway over the entire known world. Again his minister is a highly cultivated man, a philosopher who works only with inner methods. All his endeavours are aimed at ideal human goals. He seeks to establish a reconciliation between the Romans and the Goths, and anticipates a higher culture from this union. Later he withdraws completely and leads an ascetic life in a monastery.

Sagittarius and Gemini characters

Let us look at what happens if we travel by train every day. One day we find that we have plenty of time, while another day, when we have a lot to do, everything is a terrible rush. In the first case, we find that we had time to notice all sorts of things: a baby making happy noises in its pram, a beautiful flower, a bird blithely singing. In the second case, these things are virtually absent from our consciousness. All our attention is focused on a single thought: 'I must catch that train!' This idea is firmly rooted in our mind. Every fibre of our being is gripped, so that all the strength within us is subservient to that single purpose. Obviously we may not be blinded to the extent that we no longer notice the environment. For example, if it is a windy day we may be aware of the wind blowing in our face, but it merely increases our determination to conquer it with all our strength. We may also be aware of the wind behind us, but will use it only to hurry on even faster. We do not take any notice of whether it is hot or cold, wet or dry, or whether the air is sweet with the fragrance of lilac or heavy with fumes, for this will not make us move any faster or slower. In extreme cases we notice only those things which will help or hinder us, and no longer have any interest in the real meaning and value of these things.

However, it may happen that we have got the time wrong and are actually much too early. We are suddenly at peace, and the singing bird we failed to notice before can now evoke the greatest joy. We become aware of a child's efforts to attract our attention. Once we realize this, we soon discover that this sort of lost half hour is the greatest gift. We have never noticed so many things, and the world never opens up its treasury of miracles to the extent that it does when we are wandering around without any purpose.

If we rush after a single goal, we soon exert pressure on the environment. We measure our strength against it, and the environment can easily make a hostile impression. When we are granted a moment of peace, it is as if we are forced to entice the environment to come into its own as fully as possible. It is as if something friendly and with a spiritual content is radiating towards us from every side. This applies to the people we meet, but also to natural phenomena.

There are people who incessantly run after all sorts of goals, as though they are catching a train. The imagery we described in relation to the hunting centaur applies to them. There are also people who approach the whole of life more like children at play, in a way that others only do when they are granted a moment of freedom.

What is a person like when he or she runs automatically from one goal to another? We should realize that this tendency, in so far as it is a natural inclination, is based on a specific physical, mental and spiritual constitution. People like this will be intelligent and have the capacity instantly to develop an insight into difficult situations. Yet they will not be able to assess things fully and see the whole truth. This superficial assessment could be described as 'male logic.' While 'female logic' may appear to be capricious, as all sorts of subtle impressions disrupt the calm thought processes, 'male logic' can be distorted by the will. Instead of using the term 'will,' it might be better to use the word 'drive.' The insights gained may form a bastardized version of an image of the real state of affairs, and the person concerned may be in danger of viewing matters in the light of their own goals. Their thoughts seem to have some weight. They drop down all too easily into the area of the will and give rise to action without much contemplation. Thus the thoughts are actually taken over by the drive to act, and in extreme cases are almost like living creatures with all sorts of intentions. It can be rather constricting to live near such people, for even their words acquire a special weight because of the force of their thoughts, and they affect other people's wills all too easily. There is even a danger that people with a weaker nature give a sort of impression of a strong Sagittarius nature in their judgements and actions.

We may realize with a shock that the ideas of such people start to crop up in ourselves as though they were our own ideas. Moreover, their remarks may be very pointed and can therefore be extremely hurtful.

By contrast we find that, in relation to other people's views, they are sometimes extremely nervous. It is as though they are sensitive to the slightest resistance, and immediately jump to the defensive. Minor comments may seem like an attack to them, and can evoke a violent response quite out of proportion to what was said. In these situations their consciousness is extremely constricted. They are blind to everything except the one thing which they wish to reject and remove with all their might, because it seems to be in the way of their objective. It should be remembered that, for these people, achieving their own goals is the basis of their whole existence. The whole world seems worthless to them if they do not get what they want. Because they arrange and order everything around them in accordance with their goals, and therefore in a sense towards themselves just like a magnet arranges and attracts iron filings around itself, they do not notice the effect they have on others. They have no time for them, and do not consider them important, for everything outside their own plans has no weight or meaning for them. Because of their power they can cause great sorrow around them, and can involuntarily be responsible for great devastation. And yet, they can be very sensitive to their own pain. They will have a tendency to feel badly done by. While they injure others, leaving them reeling, they may feel indignant about their lack of cooperation.

Despite these difficult characteristics, they often succeed in drawing others along, and can even evoke great sympathy, although it is usually mixed with some trepidation and fear.

It is extremely important to know how to relate to such people without constantly avoiding all sorts of unbearable tensions by simply giving in to them slavishly. The worst way of responding is direct opposition, as this will merely lead to conflict and strife, evoking immeasurable strength which one will have to avoid in the end anyway, or it will lead to violent destruction. One gets the impression that such people have at their disposal an arsenal of unbounded energy. However, it is possible to get on with them as long as one accepts that within them there is a deeply concealed tension and conflict which rises up again and again in the form of strong desires. If one appeals to them from this side, and if one can approach them in a playful or in a motherly and tender way, this may be productive. It is difficult to describe precisely how to do this. Despite all their latent power we should treat them like a helpless, neglected child, entrusted to our care. If one can really succeed in adopting this attitude of motherliness, they may suddenly develop a great childlike willingness. This is expressed in an extraordinary way in a painting by Botticelli, depicting the taming of the centaur by Pallas Athene. If one can become a child again, and treat the most violent outbursts as though they were charming interludes, one may suddenly encounter a great and caring paternal aspect.

How does all this come about? There is no creature who experiences the tragedy of lost youth as profoundly as this Sagittarius character. Every creature still has a connection with the creative spiritual origin, and on the other hand, it is directed towards the environment. In everything that is young, the connection with the origin is predominant. Youth is accompanied by a carefree attitude, because it is wonderful to have so many possibilities for development, though the capacity for taking hold of the environment and controlling it is still weak. As a person reaches adulthood, the possibilities for development are lost, while the influence over the environment constantly increases. Initially everything with a potential for growth still seems to float around the growing person. He or she can still assume many different forms or traits. As they become older, only a little of their original disposition achieves external reality. The living, germinating force dies in the little that has developed.

In the nature of a Sagittarian, the capacity to influence the environment is developed to the highest degree, but the germinating force has been used up to an unusual extent. One might say that the 'inner child' is lost. This permeates the whole life of Sagittarians as a basic theme. Their decisions have such power because they direct themselves wholly to one thing, to the exclusion of all else. At the very beginning, they see deeds before them clearly outlined. In their mind they have already performed the deed before actually starting on it. Another person may start on something and then wait to see what develops from it, for the activity itself can have a creative element. On the other hand, in the Sagittarian this germinating creativity is immediately killed off. It must make way for a merciless pursuit of the goal. A well-aimed arrow is the perfect symbol for this sort of action.

From the point of view of the creation of the world, Sagittarius could be considered as the greatest and most daring experiment. Humans can be considered at their origin as being totally enveloped in the lap of divine forces. While they still consisted of a divine substance, they were scarcely distinguishable from divine figures themselves. They became increasingly separated from their origin in order to stand on their own only very gradually. But despite this separation, some of the exalted origin continues to live in them, and this is expressed in the creative urge.

In Sagittarius we encounter at the highest level the problems and possibilities resulting from this seperation. In the course of life a true Sagittarian nature will have acquired an unusually powerful share of the deepest divine substance, while at the same time the separation from his origin is greatest.

This aspect of the character is expressed in a tempestuous creative urge, and in the will to build an entirely new world. Again and again they will try to achieve something great from virtually nothing. But in doing this they feel entirely separate from the past, and this means that at any moment their creative urge can change into a tornado of destruction. What use are all those old things? They are only in the way, when Sagittarians are concerned with filling the world with their own irreplaceable expressions of their own will.

The development of such a character can only be observed with bated breath. The greatest things are alive in

it but at the same time, it is threatened by the darkest
moral shadows. For what is morality nowadays, other than
the force with which the human character, separated from
the divine, learns to orient itself once again in a divine
world order and find a place there? The greater the inner
drive, and the more complete the separation, the deeper
this morality must be to find the way. Therefore Sagittarians constantly feel as though they are standing on the
edge of an abyss. If they can find their way, they can
perform the greatest deeds. However, if the destructive
urge becomes too great, there are only two forces which can
release them from their raging; the force of the pure virgin
and the force of the child. This should never be forgotten,
no matter how wild they may be, for after all, they are
filled with the most painful longing for the virgin and
child. In the signs of the zodiac this is expressed in such a
way that the sun is in the sign of Sagittarius during
Advent, the time leading up to Christmas. Furthermore,
Sagittarius stands opposite the sign of the child, Gemini.

The Greeks found a moving way to depict this. In the
Louvre there is a statue of a centaur with a winged child
on its back, grabbing it by the hair, entitled *Centaure
dompté par l'amour* (A centaur tamed by love).

What is the opposite character in which life assumes a
form reminiscent of the unexpected waiting time for a
train? It is full of lively interest in one thing and then in
another, interested in everything, and consequently very
undirected. They constantly notice things and become
passionate about them. But one passion is soon replaced by
another, so that nothing goes very deep. They have the
capacity to displace themselves easily into other minds or
conditions, so that there can be a strong empathy without
any deep sympathy. Only a person who has taken part in
heavy and dark things in the world, or who has experienced the tragic conflict with everything which oppresses
and constrains the true human spirit can know what real
pity is. However, the person we are concerned with here

lives in a condition in which the hardships of life and its conflicts play only a minor role. These characters live in the element of light, and therefore spread a sunny happiness around them. Everything and all the events around them are new, and fascinating aspects which were never noticed before are revealed. Everything starts to shine and sparkle when they pass by, as though they are surrounded by a sunny radiance, to the extent that they can develop a healing and stimulating influence on the souls of others. They are sensitive to subtle nuances and reflect them. The finer forces of our soul open up when we come into contact with them just as they seem to make everything around them blossom. It is often as though society creates a condition in us which can only be compared with a long spell of rain, or even the darkness of winter. The Gemini type has the capacity to make the sun shine through the clouds and remove the grey veils and the cold.

However, these characters can also encounter great problems in their lives. They may develop a lively understanding of all manner of things, they may even be able to comprehend complicated interrelationships, but this does not amount to much in practice. Life remains no more than a game. For example, thought processes are more a movement of thoughts, moving to and fro between things, exchanging information, and can all too easily float above reality. Many possibilities are elicited, but as soon as a step is taken to realize a thought, a feeling of impotence may arise. The feelings also dance to and fro, and though they can flare up in great passion, even the fiercest fire will soon be extinguished. The will is constantly turned to different things, so that many tasks are undertaken, but the strength to complete them soon ebbs away leaving much unfinished. Things remain in a state rather like the condition before birth. It is hardly possible to treat matters really seriously for these characters, because it would require a gravity to which they are unable to relate, just as a butterfly cannot act like a beetle.

These characters are rarely able to take an important

decisions, for the tendency to see everything from different sides is too great, and there is little inclination to adopt just one point of view.

This can gradually lead to a sense of impotence and inner doubt. While the Sagittarius character cannot take a step without having an effect on the environment (the centaur makes the earth tremble as he passes by), the Gemini type can make extreme efforts in a practical field, without any noticeable effect. In the Sagittarius character the soul is shackled to the body, as expressed in the figure of the centaur; everything in the inner being is therefore immediately realized, one might say 'embodied' or expressed in the outer world. In the Gemini character the soul is not linked strongly enough to the body. This explains their inner mobility and lightness, as well as the inability to transform ideas into an external reality, or to give them 'body.'

In anthroposophy we find the idea that the matter comprising the human body is a condensation of the divine will. Sagittarius characters are more closely connected to this than any other creature; they owe their power to this, and their separation from the divine enables an independent creativity. In these characters there is an enormous *concentration,* and therefore they seek to be *freed* or *unshackled.* They must separate from themselves especially from the animal in them and find the connection with the divine.

In contrast, Geminis seek to be *concentrated* or *solidified.* These characters have never been wholly in control of their bodies as a tool, as they still live half in the lap of the gods. In fact, they live more in their environment than in themselves, and have not been separated from the world. They therefore run few moral risks, retaining some of their childlike disposition into adulthood. Growing up involves a need to specialize in a particular direction. As long as the soul helps to develop the body, there are still many possibilities. As the body develops, it becomes set and restricted. This is where problems arise for Gemini characters, who are aware of an infinite potential and the seeds of numerous skills, but cannot bring any of them to fruition.

In literature we often come across Sagittarius characters who play an important role. The Sagittarius-Gemini aspect also crops up frequently.

In *Zwei Menschen* by Richard Voss, the main character is a typical Sagittarian. In his youth his favourite activities include horse-riding and tireless hunting. There is a sudden break in his life when he betrays his first love. He becomes a priest, and again his whole life is directed towards a single goal: he wishes his former love to serve the Mother Church. In this man we see enormous strength and intelligence, as well as a power over other people, but his great loneliness and desire turn his whole life into a tragic hell.

The main character in Conrad Ferdinand Meyer's *Jürg Jenatsch* reveals all the Sagittarian traits in an extreme form. Again we find an inexhaustible energy and unusual intelligence, as well as the capacity to draw others on by the power of the word; again there is the strength to achieve a single goal without support, and against great opposition. In this case, his goal is the liberation of his fatherland.

The Sagittarius-Gemini mythology is clearly revealed in Felix Dahn's *Ein Kampf um Rom*. Cethegus, the Roman who wished to inspire his weakened compatriots with renewed strength to drive the Goths out of the land and restore Caesar to the throne, is a Sagittarius character through and through. He soon discovers his greatest opponent in Totila, the hero of the Goths. Strangely, his much-loved adopted son, Julius Montanus, and Totila soon discover that they are twin spirits (Montanus even has the twins as a seal). They meet because a sculptor wishes to use them as a model for Castor and Pollux, the Greek twins. Montanus, with his dark hair, reveals the more hesitant doubting side of the Gemini character; Totila, the golden-haired one reveals the irresistible sunny side to the highest degree. In Cethegus, we see all the Sagittarian traits: achieving great things from nothing, intelligence, energy, and powers of persuasion. There is a break in his life which has the effect of seperating off everything concerned with his youth. The only remaining connection is his relationship with Julius Montanus. Twice he tries to kill Totila, and both times Totila and Montanus have changed clothes, so that the weapon is aimed at Montanus. The second time, he kills Montanus by mistake. The further he pursues his goal, the more he becomes caught up in terrible moral darkness. Previously he had repeatedly betrayed his enemies to achieve his single goal, and subsequently he perpetrates the most violent acts against Christianity. His end is a total downfall.

Totila reveals the Gemini nature in a pure form. For his nature it is a joy to be chosen to be king at the moment when his kingdom is almost entirely lost. In the terrible darkness surrounding him he has the strength to develop his radiant character in the noblest way. With the help of great political skill and noble courage — but above all the moral strength of love and trust — he regains his kingdom so that it flourishes more splendidly than ever. There is something playful about his undertakings. This is show clearly when, just before his defeat, he manages to postpone a great battle for a while, and even almost brings it to a conclusion by starting to juggle brilliantly with all his weapons in the face of the enemy. This figure lives outside himself, or perhaps it is better to say, above himself. His soul is connected with the nature of the Goth people. He does not work for himself, but raises himself up so that the people can work through him. And this excessive trust is what leads to his ultimate downfall, for he does not fully understand the force of human darkness and treachery.

In this context, William Tell is also an interesting figure. He was a great archer who aimed his arrow at a child. This expresses the greatest danger, the death of a child, in a very clear image. Although the tale ends positively, it should be viewed as a powerful warning to the Sagittarian nature: 'Do not let evil tempt you to kill your child.'

The contrast between youth and its many possibilities, though still impotent in relation to the environment, and the fully grown adult who has acquired power, but has become entrenched in a single direction, can thus be seen quite clearly in relation to the characters of Gemini and Sagittarius.

The Virgo and Pisces characters

Throughout our lives we constantly encounter germination, growth and death. When an organism first germinates, the organ concerned usually has a small point-like form, such as a seed, an egg, or a bud. It has little internal structure, but still serves as a sort of gateway through which organs yet to be formed enter the realm of reality. From this single point all sorts of forms can radiate into the environment. In every germination the whole emphasis is on this movement from a centre into the world. Every seed as such is tender and sensitive, for the defence against the environment, its outline, has yet to be formed. As the organism grows, it becomes more structured, and harder and more solid. It becomes more sharply defined, and often develops thick, dead layers. But no matter how toughly such crusts or armour may protect the organism against the environment, internally they become increasingly delicate and in the core they seem to surround the new tissue with maternal care. The bud of a tree could serve as an example. In the centre there is a delicate tip where new leaves and stalks are being formed, and this is surrounded by tough, hard scales. On the outside these are smooth and resistant, but the inside is often woolly and hairy. The buds serve both as a strong protection, and as a tender, enclosure. In this way the seed of the mother organism acquires the protection which it cannot provide itself.

Thus we see again these two principles which work together: germination and enclosing. In the former, the life force radiates constantly in new forms, but the periphery is too sensitive for the rough outside world. In the latter, everything is directed outwards to protect what is developing inside. The organs used for this protection have little potential for further development, but serve to allow the development of a new beginning.

In cultural life there is also a constant interaction between the process of germination and that which protects this germination. For example, this applies to the development and care of children. It is immediately clear that the germinating potential within children can only develop with the protection of the mother and of the whole family. And this is not all. A great deal of what seems to happen automatically in nature does not work so well for human beings. Plants choose and process their own food, and organize their protection against the environment themselves, but all this is much more difficult for human beings. If a human child is to develop fully it is important not only to pay attention to the environment, but also to facilitate and stimulate the development of its skills. In child-rearing there are two main tasks. On the one hand there is the task of a sower: the child is given many things which may serve to bring about an inner awakening, a kind of spiritual germination. Children are directed in their experiences and are required to perform certain activities. On the other hand, they must be given space and an atmosphere in which they can flourish, so that all inborn or learned skills can develop. One must withdraw, but continue to surround children with love, and ensure that harmful influences are kept at bay.

The two functions of germination and protection not only occur in nature, but also in social life.

It may be a long time before a Virgo character is revealed clearly. It may be useful to remember the bud and its development to understand these characters better. While obviously the Virgo character may be a man or a woman, we will describe it as feminine in accordance with the sign of the zodiac.

These characters have involuntarily made a sharp distinction between their own world and the outside world. They will be very careful and tender with everything in their own world, but there is a tendency to reject the outside world revealing a strange contrast between tenderness and hardness.

For example, one may meet someone who gives an impression of having something very beautiful inside. This aspect may be very attractive, and one is tempted to approach it. But what happens? Unexpectedly, there is an impression of icy coldness. One may even be unreasonably and painfully rejected, and this can cause great inner pain.

If one has a good friend who is a Virgo character character, and visits her while suffering inner trouble, one would expect to be warmly welcomed. Again it may seem as though the entire friendship is meaningless, and there is nothing but coldness. One feels coldly rejected in the midst of one's troubles, and yet the friendship may be no less strong.

One expects loving feelings from the Virgo character, but the opposite is all too common: an inability to feel sympathy or to share another's troubles. One may be used to talking to others about one's ideas, for it is well-known that the interaction which occurs in such discussions can have an extremely fruitful effect. However, if one talks to a Virgo character about things which are of the utmost importance, she may be unable to respond. She cannot empathize or exert any fruitful influence.

However, one should not expect a Virgo to do this. She can only be approached by a sort of inner journey. We should never expect her to approach us. She is always ahead of us. She is like a distant country which arouses deep longings in us, because she protects a supernatural wonder. Sometimes we succeed in reaching this distant wondrous area, and we feel safe and protected by great maternal feelings. Then one knows that this is the most heavenly feeling on earth. But even then one may be very easily rejected. If one makes the slightest mistake, this character feels that her deep inner order is threatened, and suddenly one is confronted again by a cold wall. The wondrous aspect one had discovered is once again infinitely distant.

A Virgo character is almost incapable of visiting anyone else, and when visiting her it is important to keep very strictly to the house rules, or the door will be shut. She is entirely concerned with receiving, but then only really with receiving children. If we wish to enter, we must also offer something childlike, something she can protect, look after and help to develop. If we act strongly and make demands, she will withdraw and hide, shutting the door behind her. But when there is something tender and unsure in us, something unguarded and so sensitive that it is as though we are asking a silent question, it is as though the door opens again, and we can enter into heaven.

It is also possible to be more superficial with her, but then we have to behave as though we are visiting to admire her child. In other words, we must be prepared to take a great interest in her affairs before we can expect anything else.

It can be surprising to see that this Virgo character seems to have little sense of responsibility in certain areas, even when she is morally scrupulous in other aspects. However, this becomes understandable when we realise that she views the environment as an outside world which must be kept away from the area which is important to her. How can one feel responsibility for something unimportant, or even hostile?

All these difficult qualities mentioned above can be understood in this light. If we go to her with our own problems or make demands, she sees us as coming from the outside world. If she were to open up to this, she would experience this as a form of pollution.

She is protective towards her inner self, for she has something very precious to look after and protect, and her task must be fulfilled.

How does this character feel? She has an urge to devote

herself to a single task, and this becomes her whole world. If this one thing — whether it is someone she loves, a child, a family, or some other task in life — has not materialized, she experiences a profound feeling of inner suffering and longing. She feels a sense of impotence, for she must wait; she cannot seek it. If she fails to find something to fulfil her, she may become bitter and dried up (Virgo becomes a spinster).

In general, her spiritual forces may be expected to bear the stamp of her inner world: everything is bright, transparent and well ordered. Everything has its own place, so that it can calmly develop. As a rule, she may be intelligent and receptive, but not very productive. She seems withdrawn, cool and detached when dealing with worldly matters. Her judgments on important decisions may be strict, and perhaps even hard, for everything is compared to her inner ideal. In a less strongly developed Virgo character the judgment may be based on prejudice or preconceived ideas. Thus there is little that can stand up against it, and the rest collapses. But if her thoughts are directed at something she has inwardly accepted, they may be filled with a great intimacy. The important thing is her emotional life, as described in detail above.

Perhaps this is the place to mention another curious aspect. As a rule, the true Virgo character does not explain herself enough. She demands that other people immediately understand her. She experiences everything so intensely that she always feels she must have expressed herself. This lack of explanation can make things difficult for people around her. Her will is characterized by reticence and by the tendency not to exert any outward strength. She is completely taken up with protecting certain things so that they can develop in a sheltered place. In that place she ensures the strictest order and routine.

There are people who have such an abundant inner life that the whole outside world seems like arid soil which they want to plant and water. Their inner wealth is not felt as their own. For them it is more as though they are managing it on behalf of others. It is characterized by great sensitivity, so that the inner poverty of others makes a strong impression on them. Their whole nature is dominated by a sort of pity. It may be a very noble quality, but this is not always the case. It is quite possible that the pity is directed at transient impressions and may be too superficial to note any real distress.

The real problem of the Pisces character lies in another direction. The feeling that they have too much and want to give their riches to others is due to the constitution of their life forces. An aspect of these flows outwards, constantly welling up. While the Virgo character is well aware of the limits of her domain and scope, and will not easily confuse her own domain with that of another, the constitution of the Pisces character is not so outlined and has little outward reticence or restrictions. They like to be generous with money, and in general will allow others to use their possessions, but they will also tend to use other's possessions all too readily. They lack a certain ability to distinguish, because everything flows together in them. They are not very careful or ordered outwardly, and the same applies to their inner life. Their mental and emotional forces tend to blend together. There is no strict inner order. This can also be illustrated with a bud of a plant. Every germinating part is undifferentiated and the structures and distinctions only become apparent when the plant grows. This character's thoughts may be rather hazy, and even dreamy. They may also be excessively imaginative. In general, the domain of thought is the deadest and most abstract aspect of our inner life. But in the Pisces character, this area is also permeated with life forces. It follows that there is a strong productive urge, particularly in the artistic field. In general, such thoughts — which are full of life — have a fruitful effect on other people. Therefore this leads to an urge to participate and do good.

This thinking is not very different from feeling. In characteristic cases, thinking occurs in images which are borne by the waves of the emotions. Pisceans carry their hearts in their heads. It is clear that with this type of thinking it is not easy to penetrate abstract forms of thinking which do not rely on imagery, such as algebra, for instance. The Piscean may have a comprehensive power of thinking, and yet be rather unintelligent in this particular area.

The emotional life of Pisceans tends to be very tender. Again they will not make a sharp distinction between what is accepted and what is rejected. Therefore they are not harsh judges. They tend to sympathize with everything, whether it is good or bad, of a high or of a low quality.

Their will is directed towards seeking, helping and influencing others. Pisceans would like to drain themselves. We will see below how this can lead to either very elevated or very base results.

The fact that they are unable to concentrate on a single matter can lead to great difficulties for the Pisces character. They have a tendency to be involved with many different things at the same time. This is caused particularly by seeing the environment as being too influential. This could be viewed as a lack of concentration. This characteristic, coupled with the tendency to attach little importance to personal matters, can lead to terrible untidiness.

In literature we often come across the theme of the virgin on the river bank. This is always indicative of a great inner search, a yearning for unattainable distances. One of the best examples of this is Goethe's *Iphigenie*. Another example is the *Fritjof Saga*. There is usually a man who sails away or arrives. When we examine the imagery, it is clear that there is a link between fish and navigation, particularly with sailing. The eternal motion storming onwards without any holding back, wandering into the distance — are all characteristic of this.

However, there is another aspect of the Piscean character which is expressed both in myth and in nature. This is the loyalty to their origins, or at least the urge to rediscover their origins. This instinct is most evident in salmon and eels. To reproduce, salmon always find the stream where they were born. And eels return to the Sargasso Sea to spawn.

The German mystic, Rulman Merswim, described the development of man in images strongly reminiscent of the migration of salmon. A number of fish live in waters high up in the rocky mountains. They start to fight and swim to the edge of the rocks to drop down with the water. They descend from waterfall to waterfall, ever further down, and eventually come to a sea where they all go their own way. However, they then return and travel back up to the heights. Their tremendous struggle is described in moving images. Many fish are crushed as they jump up the water-falls. Finally, some succeed in returning to their place of origin. They are now a different colour. Many are caught on the way, and these turn black.

This description from the beginning of our own cultural era echoes the era's traditional character of a fish, because the spring equinox currently falls in Pisces. This can provide guidelines for man's conduct in our time. We have moved a long way from our origins and have wandered around the world. It is now time to journey back to our origins. The black fish and those that died indicate that in this task we are threatened with great danger.

Perhaps there is no more striking image of the loss of a link with our native country and our divine origins than the story of the Flying Dutchman. We are all living in this condition. We have been left to the restlessness of the environment and to raging storms all around us. This story emphasizes the search for land, the desire for our native country. The clearest description of the interaction with the Virgo character is given in Wagner's version. Salvation comes only after meeting a virgin who is waiting for the hero and is true to him until death. A similar dramatic intensity is found in the images of Rulman Merswim as in the *Flying Dutchman*. The name of the story indicates for the Dutch people that they are profoundly involved with the problems of shipping and fish. In fact, some of the most important myths and legends for the Dutch people contain this theme of a river-bank. For example, one of the Lohengrin stories is set both on the Rhine and on the Scheldt.

In the *Flying Dutchman* the virgin is nobly fulfilling her great task, but in the Lohengrin story there is a noble lady who is constantly assailed by evil influences. In the strange fairy-tale, *The Lady of Stavoren,* the lady concerned reveals a problematic side of her nature: pride in possessions. She seeks outward show or splendour. She does not recognize the ethereal gold radiating from a child, and rejects the living gold of wheat. She not only wants to protect her world, but also wants it to exceed all others. Finally, her downfall is announced in the form of a dead fish with her own ring in its belly.

The gifts that the fish can bring from its watery world is hinted at in some folk tales. In 'The Two fishermen's Sons' the beginning of the fairy-tale describes the two constellations — Virgo-Pisces and Sagittarius-Gemini. It is significant that the fisherman's wife gives birth to twins after serving up a magical fish to her husband. Here the fish is the image of something unborn, something which wishes to be born. The water in which the fish lives represents the pre-birth world, or the realm of life forces out of which living creatures emerge to form solid figures.

The virgin on the river-bank represents the female essence which is open for the unborn child to descend into. It is important to understand this, as it expresses a central question for the Dutch nation. In purely geographic terms, the Dutch are people of the shore and could perhaps even be described as a nation seeking land. The national character, of an abundance of unused or unborn life forces, is related to this.

The Capricorn and Cancer characters

To characterize this pair, let me describe a situation which was common during the war. A lecturer's or preacher's job was to represent certain ideas in lectures or sermons. On occasion they had to travel and spend nights away from home. At one point it seemed an invasion was imminent, and trains were being shot at. What should they do? If something were to happen, they could be killed, or they might be unable to reach their family. This could lead to a personal tragedy. If, however, they did not travel, they would be failing in their task, which might result in other people losing certain inner possibilities. Of course, in most cases their worries would have been unnecessary.

In one case the spiritual task comes first, even though this may entail risking one's own life and the family's safety. In the other case, one chooses for physical safety and well-being, and abandons the fulfilment of the spiritual task.

There are people for whom it is obvious to choose the careful solution, and others who like to take a risk. The former always try to keep their feet on firm ground; the latter like to leap dangerously over abysses.

The true Cancer character always chooses the careful solution. Their whole life is aimed at avoiding risks and dangers. Why should they jeopardise everything they feel sure of — their life, their health, their possessions, their reputation — for things which seem a matter of the imagination, such as anything which transcends physical reality? They are very good at looking after themselves and their family, and that is enough. There are only a few important matters in life, and the rest follows automatically: a roof over your head, a good income providing good food, and solid prospects for the future. In fact, it would even be better if people did not have individual inner lives, as this merely disturbs the existing situation. It would be simplest if everyone kept strictly to traditional moral values and behaved sensibly. Of course, a little bit of religion is fine, for that's as it should be, and it may be a good idea to do something about it, for you never know what follows this life.

It will be clear that as they grow older, many people have more and more Cancerian characteristics. This is one of the reasons why young people often feel misunderstood, and it leads to many problems and a lack of direction.

Self-awareness is rather difficult for the Cancer character. This is actually a spiritual matter. To be truly self-aware, human beings must consider themselves as spiritual beings at an inner level. This concept is utterly alien to the Cancerian. They can only base their self-awareness on things which have reality for them and these are mainly external material things. Above all, they feel a sense of growth as their possessions grow. Possessing a family means a great deal to them. This is not so much related to the fulfilment of deep ideals, for they have little need for far-reaching interaction. They feel that the family is something to which they can direct their abilities: regular daily work, a caring attitude, precautions, thrift, sensible management, orderliness. Their self-esteem is strongly dependent on other people's opinions. As the average expectation is not very high, they often accept fairly low standards.

The same values by which they judge themselves also apply for other people. They also weigh more for them if they possess more, have better prospects, and behave properly. Thus they often make mistakes about people.

The world as observed through the eyes of this character tends to be rather colourless and undifferentiated. Their observation is rather like a sort of probing, touching movement. They do little more than carefully touch things, even when using their eyes and ears. They make a note of what there is, and then withdraw. After all, in order to penetrate the real quality of things, it would be necessary for them to come out of themselves and to enter into the object. They therefore get little joy from their observations. As they have little understanding of the things around them, they are very prone to vague anxieties of concealed dangers.

These characters only feel really safe when it is possible to approach things in terms of their size, number and weight — the very aspects which are of least importance regarding their true nature. Therefore they will not readily arrive at independent insights. There are no other characters with so little sense for profound truths. They assess things in practical and purely quantitative terms, and are mainly concerned with how they might be helpful for survival, and how to stave off damaging influences. They use their thoughts rather like pincers, grasping the world for their own purposes without really penetrating it.

In this respect they are inclined to think in terms of how much things are worth. To them a cow and a painting are more or less the same, if they both cost a thousand pounds. Nevertheless, differences still remain, and there may even be a difference between two paintings of the same value: one may be larger or heavier, which could be relevant when shipping or hanging it! If you show the typical Cancerian a painting, he or she will be primarily interested in how much it is worth, then who painted it, and finally, what people think of it. When they know all this, they can make a judgment.

Emotionally Cancerians live between a sense of fear and a feeling of comfort. They appreciate everything which contributes to a sense of well-being, security and equanimity. On the other hand, everything which threatens this is disliked and quickly rejected.

The will is mainly concerned with performing mundane everyday tasks with great care. If the will is stronger, Cancerians will aim for a better position, based on greater income and possessions. They are prepared to make great efforts to maintain and ensure their own well-being and that of their family.

Despite this description, one should not think that the Cancer character behaves in any way unpleasantly. They can be very friendly and easy-going, and in a sense even generous, for they like everyone to have what they deserve. They will also be happy to talk about all sorts of subjects, but their conversation consists of one commonplace remark after another. They never express an original idea, but only those which they have heard around them.

Our western society reveals that many people have Cancerian characteristics. The bourgeois character, or upright citizen, is very similar to the Cancer character. For a long time humankind has turned away from the cosmos and towards the earth. It is not surprising that man is dominated by this sign, in which the sun begins on its descent into the depths.

While the Aquarius character, who has a special link with the whole zodiac, cannot really act purely in accordance with his character in our society, the Cancer character will find all the conditions to develop fully. This character also has an important task to fulfil in the ring of the twelve signs, but nowadays it has proliferated to such an extent that it has become a cultural disease. This Cancer has become a cancerous growth in society. There are a number of unpleasant phenomena which are symptomatic of this cancerous disease. It is rather sad that these matters are considered perfectly normal.

It is obviously good to take care and look after things, and to save and acquire a basis of security for times when one may no longer be strong enough to earn a living. However, the huge growth of life insurance companies is symptomatic of a widespread fear of life. We feel the future has an indeterminate character, and it should have this character. Courage is needed to cope with this. However, many people wish to plan the way to the future quite firmly, even though this can often be at the expense of the full experience of the present moment. Much of that which is seen as religion is no more than a rather sophisticated form of life insurance. Only in this case, the payment for a good life is made after death.

Scientific materialism is a pure breeding ground for

Cancerian tendencies. Many people have great difficulty trying to escape from this. Science has a tendency to approach everything in terms of size, weight and number, and to ignore qualitative considerations. There is also a tendency to turn away from higher aspects, or even to deny their existence. Again the fear of losing a firm footing plays a significant role. An attempt is made to represent things in such a way that they are firmly held like solid objects. Instead of pursuing the truth, scientists juggle with theory. All great theories are merely mental constructions, and are periodically dismissed. It is a historical image, suspiciously like the constricting shell that is periodically cast off during the life cycle of a crab. One might even view the great theories like a series of hard shells for repelling the awesome and overwhelming truth. The attitude to materialism is characteristic. Over the last centuries the whole worldview gradually became based upon a very dry and solid representation of matter. Suddenly with the splitting of the atom, this matter appears to contain an abyss. This is a surprise which seems more suitable for a Capricorn.

Another Cancerian symptom is the desire for spiritual beings which can actually only be encountered at an extra-sensory level to be revealed in the sensory world, as in spiritualist seances and the like. Here the spirit is not denied, but it is dragged down and materialized.

Finally, we would like to mention one other typical characteristic of the Cancerian character which also applies to our time as a whole. As these people are primarily interested in the well-being of their own body, they try to avoid anything related to death or ageing. They would like a world in which there is only birth and growth. Therefore they also fail to harvest the fruits of age. In the past we saw that the development of consciousness occurred at the expense of processes of decay. A true culture coupled with profound wisdom can only flourish where the forces of death are taken seriously. In our time, it is as though death has assumed an extra large and completely uncontrollable power because it is rejected.

In summary the Cancerian characteristics tend towards the same direction: seeking support in the lower regions and attempting to materialise higher intangible aspects in such a way that they offer as much support as solid things. This is another aspect of the descending sun's arc. However, what should merely be a movement *through* the depths, becomes a movement *into the depths*. The love of material goods and the external world becomes a prison.

People with the Capricorn character find it difficult to tolerate the routine of daily life. They are not suited to living a bourgeois life, for this is based on regular meals on the table, mending the roof as soon as it leaks, lighting the fire when it gets cold, and switching the light on when it is dark. Everything happens more or less automatically. Salaries, or the dividend on stocks and shares are paid regularly, and the rent is also paid out regularly. However, this life is like a treadmill, either in the household itself, or in work outside the home. These demand almost all the strength one has for things in which one has little interest, leaving very little strength or time for one's own personal life.

True Capricorns do not wish to be fed in a safe home. They want to take risks, constantly jeopardising their whole existence, and in this way encounter the most exhilarating experiences. They do not wish to lean on tradition or on a system, but entirely on their own strength and insight. They are only happy in the greatest danger for they only feel their full strength in this situation, and are then able to develop great presence of mind.

The extreme Cancerian is satisfied when merely the body is alive; the Capricorn would like to be all spirit and mind. They feel utter contempt for any physical restraints, for heaviness, tiredness and illness. It sometimes happens that these people are in extremely difficult situations, but do not pity them straightaway. Looking carefully, it may be clear that they would not wish it otherwise, for life is giving them an opportunity to experience something, and to test themselves and their own strength.

There is no doubt that there are many people who only felt really good in the impossible situations which occurred in the war, because they were finally wrenched out of their bourgeois lives and could lead a dangerous and uncertain existence in hiding, or as members of a secret organization. Of course, this does not in any way detract from the great importance of their work, nor should it be seen as a criticism of their motives. It is merely a description of the inner experience of certain people.

What are people of the Capricorn character looking for? They wish to be free of the whole of the rest of the world. There is no doubt that many of the greatest achievements of humankind have been attained by people with a Capricorn temperament. They dare to climb the most difficult mountains and explore unknown territory. The term 'dare' is not really accurate, for they are actually stimulated by danger. They will undergo the greatest poverty if this means that they can produce great works of art. But at the same time they are people who can easily bring themselves and their families to ruin. Children with a Capricorn parent may have difficulties later in life: they could have a rather weak constitution for the rest of their life if they had to suffer hunger because of an impulsive Capricorn father. Or children may have to bury their misery in loneliness, for a Capricorn mother has too many other interests. This may result in a life of indecision, and it would not be surprising if these children started following some strange paths, for it is difficult to hold a steady course without solid moral norms.

While it is always a problem for a Cancerian to maintain the necessary self-awareness, the self-awareness of a Capricorn is more of a problem for others. A Cancerian's toes may seem like long antennae, but the Capricorn sometimes has a tendency to stamp toes in a lively way. Their whole consciousness is concentrated on the self, and therefore their attitude is often superior and conceited. A true Capricorn character is driven by pride to fight for the highest things they can achieve. The primitive Capricorn nature will contemptuously knock down everything around them so that they can still look over others.

In any case, they are against tradition and authority. This can result in all sorts of strange leaps and bounds, but also in powerful insights. They are totally original. Their whole interest is aimed at individual aspects, also of other people. They try to capture their own spiritual self and to discover the spiritual side of other people. It is a high Capricorn ideal to live as a spirit among other spirits. The observations of a Capricorn character are strongly related to the will. There is a constant challenge rather like a trial of strength, with the question: 'Can I overcome you, or are you too powerful for me?' One is reminded again and again of the fanatic mountaineer facing an unclimbed peak. This may be an outward challenge, so that every resistance becomes a literal trial of strength, but there may also be an inner call for the highest achievements. However, whether they are facing inner or outer challenges, Capricorns always act as though they are facing powers against which they must measure themselves, and which must not defeat them.

Perhaps certain great explorers and conquerors achieved so much because they felt not only the challenge posed by the vast continents, but were also able to relate to whole regions and nations as though they were relating to tremendous spiritual forces.

The Capricorn character also reveals this trait of the trial of strength and the refusal to retreat from anything in their thoughts. They start from the point in which man transcends all other creatures; their basis lies in the possibility of achieving freedom. They seek first of all those things which come last for other people. They are attracted to the deepest places in the world where spiritual creatures are beginning to differentiate themselves. To them the rest of the world is no more than the interaction between spiritual beings moving of their own accord. The Capricorn character's greatest instinct is to forge his or her own spiritual being, and as such, interact with the spiritual beings at the most profound level.

Goethe's Faust acts in a truly Capricorn style when he stands opposite the sign of the macrocosm and calls up the earth spirit. In contrast, Wagner's Famulus reveals traits which are not entirely unlike those of the Cancerian character.

If the Capricorn character is less noble, his or her thinking will tend to be rather capricious. It is still original, but contains some incomprehensible leaps. Nevertheless, surprising aspects may arise from all the strange thoughts.

In their emotional life, courage and a love of danger, combat and fighting are predominant. There is a great dislike of any form of daily routine. In an ignoble character this can lead to an unbridled desire for sensationalism, but in its highest form it becomes a search for heroic deeds. In the will, conquering everything which impinges from outside plays a great role. The most typical characteristic of the Capricorn will is perhaps their readiness to constantly gamble their whole existence for the highest stake.

Although we should adopt an impartial and businesslike attitude towards all the signs of the zodiac as we are studying them, it is only natural that, even when acting very positively, the Cancerian character does not evoke much sympathy or admiration. It is actually the Capricorn character which evokes the greatest admiration.

In Felix Dahn's *Ein Kampf um Rom* Teja, the last king of the Goths, is depicted as a great hero. He reveals strong Capricorn traits. Everyone else still holds on to some illusion which serves as a base for the whole of life. From the very beginning, Teja is convinced that the Goths have lost the struggle on earth, and that there is no consolation for them in heaven. And yet, he achieves more than anyone else in the fight, simply because he sees this as being necessary for human dignity. It is precisely because he sees the abyss of the downfall as the only perspective that he has the possibility of showing that true man has a source of strength which can conquer the whole world.

The other king, Theodahad, serves as a sort of counterpart. He is completely dominated by the fear of losing his life and the desire to acquire possessions. Dahn characterizes him, and the Cancerian character, in a brilliant short description. When he is threatened by defeat, he says: '... there's nothing like flight' and later: 'and life is still about money.'

Here the Cancerian character is seen in a very dark light. The most dreadful avarice is the result of his tendency to hold on to his life and his possessions at all costs. Others are exploited without mercy. He even sells the whole kingdom for which other people have laid down their lives. It is not so much that he is acting with cruelty in this, but that he does not recognize the spirituality in other people, and is therefore totally unable to empathize with them. Other people's suffering is outside the experience of this character.

Conrad Ferdinand Meyer also described the Cancer/Capricorn duality characteristically in *Gustaph Adolf's Page*. In this case the tension between the two characters is not as great. In the Leubelfing father and son, the fear and competition for possession do play an important role, though they are not entirely blinded by these aspects. Their respective niece and cousin, the page, does reveal great courage coupled with a desire for sensation, but she does not achieve great heroism. This is characteristic; in her career as a page she gambles her life to achieve a high point. Meyer points to her life summarizing the essence of these questions in brief sentences. For example, the motto of the page is *'Courte et bonne.'* In contrast, the Cancerian character would have to say: 'Boredom is unimportant; just let it go on.' At the end, someone says to the young Leubelfing: 'You have saved your highest goal, dear life itself. That will keep you happy.' The fact that he lost his name and his identity is unimportant to him.

The Aries and Libra characters

In a group of people having a discussion there will be those
who are personally involved in the subjects being discussed, while others are merely enjoying being together.

The former will have a tendency to put their views
forward sharply and incisively, and to oppose or reject
every counter argument, even intimidating some of the
group to silence. If they are deeply concerned about the
subject, it is almost as though they are hammering on the
anvil of truth.

The latter will not put forward their own views so
strongly, but will be more concerned with ensuring the
right interaction between those present. The statements
made by any particular person are not considered very
important; the process taking place in the group is considered more significant. They may jump to someone's defence, in spite of their own view if they feel that the person
is not putting his or her opinion forward with sufficient
strength. This ensures that everyone is involved in the
discussion, and the subject has been examined from every
side. It is even possible that they will bring up an aspect
not represented by anyone, and which does not even concur
with their own view, so that the subject has been truly
covered from every angle.

True Aries characters are convinced that they should
forcefully put forward their own views. They behave as
though they are bearing a strong light in a world of darkness. They feel an urge to shine their light on everything.
They always have certain views, or sometimes just one
view, which they believe will help things around them, or
even improve the whole world. They are never satisfied
with gaining an insight into things, but always want others
to have this view as well. They wish to share their views
and convince others, and are only satisfied when they are
able to change things around them.

When something goes wrong, they tend to feel this

personally, even when it has nothing to do with them. Therefore they are inclined to take on enormous responsibilities. Very often this is only expressed in a sense of irritation and critical remarks. For example, this happens when they see somebody doing something badly, or breaking the traffic rules. Their full fighting spirit is aroused when they feel a need to protect the weak. For example, they will intervene if they notice anyone tormenting animals, and will move heaven and earth when they become aware of injustice. An inventor who takes every risk to develop his or her invention, without expecting any personal gain, is characteristic of the Aries nature. The inventor sees a need and decides how to satisfy it, wishing to innovate on the basis of an idea. The true Aries character is never selfish in the ordinary sense. They do not act for their own gain, and sometimes even do things against their own interests. They will jeopardise their physical safety and well-being, as well as that of their family. They care little about these things, and are therefore able to suffer great hardships. However, in a more subtle way they can be self-seeking, for they seek the satisfaction which comes from the recognition of their ideas, even at the expense of others.

The style of thinking of the Aries character has a rock-like quality. Because of the strong will which is part of their thinking, the latter has very sharp and a rather inflexible outline. The ideas in their mind can become so concentrated that they are almost like solid objects. This 'thought object,' which is loaded with a strong will, has a tendency to lead to a sort of obsession. Aries characters cannot rest until everything that is in their mind has been expressed and has an effect on the environment.

There is a similarity between the Aries and the Sagittarius character. However, the Sagittarian is always concerned with achieving a particular goal, or building up something totally new. It is not particularly important how this is achieved, or what other people think about it. Sagittarians builds on nothing. They seek absolutely new ground. Arians are usually concerned with renewing or improving something which has deteriorated. They do all they can to make other people recognize their convictions.

The emotions of the Aries character reveal a tendency to judge. They constantly apply strong moral standards and makes high demands. In all their encounters they make harsh black and white distinctions. Anything that does not look pure white is vehemently rejected, and anything that looks pure white is accepted. (It is interesting to note that sheep are also either black or white, and are rarely spotted.) The Aries character has a tendency to fanaticism in every field. They always apply rigid and fixed norms, and have little capacity for tact. Because of their will, this character also has the quality of a smith or a soldier. They will hammer the anvil with extraordinary toughness, but may also try to break the cold iron with their hands.

They will always serve a goal, but not in the sense of the Taurean serving another person, or an accepted idea. It is their own idea or conviction which is of the greatest importance to them, and for which they are ready to jeopardise everything.

While Arians act on the assumption that the world will benefit if their convictions are achieved, people with the Libra character are convinced that everything that is important already exists in the world. In any case, they consider the world and the achievements of man so impressive that they do not feel they can easily add anything to it. Yet they are certainly aware that things go wrong — or at least, that everything is not as it could be. However, they ascribe this to a lack of balance, and the fact that various forces are not in equilibrium. The Aries character has some of the traits of an inventor; the Libra character, those of a repairer. The former could be called a pathfinder; the other tends more to maintain the path.

People with the Libra character do not consider themselves to be important, and in particular do not attach a great deal of importance to their own convictions, although they do want to achieve important things. They believe that if they are able to create a harmonious interaction, others will ensure that good things happen. As we saw earlier, in a discussion they are unlikely to put their own view forward very forcefully. However, they will come to the aid of someone who represents his or her view rather weakly, so that it gets the attention it deserves. Libras do not really expect anything from one person alone, but they expect a great deal from the careful and common consideration of a question by several people, or more clearly, from all those who are concerned with a particular matter.

When two people are both dominant and have explicit views leading to violent clashes and conflict, the Libra character comes into its own. It is only then that they truly wake up and become active. They immediately see every imminent misunderstanding, and will try to clear it up. They will do all they can to obtain the mutual recognition of the two points of view, thus enabling a healthy exchange. They find it extremely easy to understand the viewpoints of other people, and can recognize their value. By giving equal weight to every point of view, they operate in an atmosphere of tact.

The above clearly shows the weak side of the Libra character. In them the outside world has an excessively important role as a standard for their actions, and the inner world is unimportant. This can easily lead to a weak character and a tendency to go with the flow. They must also fight against a tendency to be rather slow. They constantly have to be roused by the outside world, and only operate at full strength when they are given a lot to bear and to assimilate. In comparison, for the Aries character, the inner world sets a dominant standard, and this character tends to be too rigid, irritated by slowness and always active.

The thinking of the Libra character has a contemplative quality. This is less difficult for Librans than for others as they have little need for tangible results. 'Weighing things up' is a term which accurately expresses their thinking. The pros and the cons of any matter, and the probable final result, are examined carefully. These characters find it difficult to draw conclusions or judge other people when their good and bad qualities are both apparent. There is never any tendency to insist on anything, to say, 'This is how it is,' but always, 'It might be like this, or it might be like that.' The style of thinking is not necessarily vague, but is so flexible that one idea or view can easily be replaced by another.

The emotions of the Libra character particularly reflect this position in the middle of everything, a sort of organ of equilibrium for the feelings. These characters immediately become aware of disturbed relationships, and this arouses a certain antipathy in them. Everything is related to this feeling of inner harmony, which is based on cosmic relationships. Therefore these characters are not very critical, and their dislikes are not very strong. Their sympathies are also less strong than those of the Aries character. Their will is always concerned with creating flexible and harmonious relationships everywhere. In their view, a propelling force for change is adequately provided by other people. Therefore one should not expect them to perform any concrete tasks. When something is going well, they wish to keep it going and arrange things in such a way that they continue as well as possible.

Some impressive examples of the Aries and Libra characters can again be found in *Ein Kampf um Rom*. Hildebrand, Theoderik's faithful retainer, acts entirely in accordance with the Aries character. This is indicated symbolically when he is in charge of a battering ram during the siege of Rome. Witichis, one of the kings, displays a pair of scales on his standard, and behaves entirely as a Libran. Throughout the fierce battle he always considers matters carefully and calmly. He is not so much a leader as someone who is happy to take great responsibility. When there is an important court case, he represents the defendants entirely against his own convictions and against the views of everybody present, simply because he believes that justice and reason should prevail, even in the worst cases.

Hildebrand is the great leader. He calls on his comrades to lead the nation and arouse it. He is the force behind the battle, and constantly hammers at the need for the Goths to rely on their own strength if they are not to go under. Unconditionally he allows his grandson to be put to death, the only remaining member of his family who took the side of the Romans. He was the one who demanded the greatest sacrifice in the interests of the nation, with the extreme severity of Witichis. He is also the one who always looks back to the past (the ram's head looking back), while giving others the impetus to move on.

6. The Zodiac and the Art of Living

Dangers and possibilities

The more we examine ourselves and animals, the more we discover that everything which takes place in an animal can also be found in ourselves. And yet there are enormous differences in the way in which these forces operate.

Animals are completely assimilated into nature's tapestry of wisdom, so that all their actions, even the most conscious actions, are determined by and aimed at something of which they remain unaware.

By contrast, human beings have been virtually torn free of this tapestry of natural wisdom with respect to their thoughts, feelings and actions. Therefore it is possible for them to act on their own insights. They may be fully aware of the guidelines which apply to their actions, but this is only the case if they allow their own thoughts to assume the role which is played by the wisdom of nature for animals. Only those activities to which this fully applies can really be termed human activities.

However, man can also be unconsciously directed by forces in him which correspond to those operating in animals. Strangely this very often leads to actions which conflict with all established wisdom.

Moral standards can never be applied to an animal. It is unable to act any differently, and its acts correspond to the natural area in which it belongs. It is actually an organ of a single, world-encompassing entity of wisdom, which is incapable of violating the natural order.

In contrast, the life of virtually every person is full of violations of various degrees. Although we have the possibility of elevating ourselves to a pure reflection of truth in our thinking, there are numerous illusions, injustices and falsehoods in our minds. While our feelings are inclined to explore and become part of a single large world, a communal harmony, we are constantly coming up against the world order. A pure will is a total renunciation of the self. If we were able to renounce ourselves, we would surrender to the realization which lights up in us as wisdom. On the other hand, conflicts and disorder often follow from our acts. Many of our activities conflict with the world's needs.

All these wrongnesses occur particularly when we do not consciously direct our activities but merely follow what in the animals world is infallible instinct.

Not only has humankind abandoned wisdom in a conscious sense, it has also unconsciously surrendered to a counter wisdom that opposes world harmony.

Rudolf Steiner pointed out many times that strong forces affect man, opposing the just course of world development. In keeping with ancient traditions he called these forces 'Luciferian' and 'Ahrimanic' beings. In the New Testament they are referred to as the Devil and Satan.

This brings us to one of the greatest enigmas: what is the purpose and what is the origin of evil?*

What would happen to man if these forces did not operate? If this were the case, our thoughts, feelings and will would contain only divine aspects. It would not occur to us ever to do anything impulsive or to have a single absurd thought. The divine forces would feel, think and will in us. We would be no more than organs within the world as a whole, as are the animals, albeit at a higher level.

Rudolf Steiner described how in ancient times elevated divine beings released certain other beings from their authority. The latter developed in a different way from the former. They felt increasingly separate from normal development, and became opponents of the beings, who

* This subject is explored further in Alfred Schütze's *The Enigma of Evil,* Floris Books, Edinburgh 1978.

continued to work on the evolution of the world in a positive way, hindering their development.

These obstructive beings intervened in the development
of humankind in a way that was inappropriate at that
stage, but would have been was appropriate for a previous
era. This resulted in all sorts of shifts. In this way, humankind became increasingly separate from direct divine
guidance, and was influenced in a way which did not allow
it to reach its full potential. In the Old Testament these
events are described in the Fall and the Expulsion from
Paradise.

Thus humankind became a stage for the constant battle
between divine and counter-divine powers. But this created
the possibility for the development of an inner human self
with a completely independent inner world. All sorts of
external influences affect this, but they can be repelled or
assimilated. Everything that is used for independent
thought must be acquired. When the will is guided in
particular activities only by the insights that have been
acquired, the activity is not influenced by anything else; it
is quite independent. At that moment the whole being is
acting in an independent way.

As a result of the influence of these obstructive powers,
man is able to turn away from the divine and be influenced
by evil. However, the whole purpose of this is that man is
able to act freely.

Human beings have become creatures with their own
inner creative centres. In the story of paradise God expressed this as follows: 'See, man has become one of us,
knowing good and evil.' Therefore man's freedom is dependent on the very existence of evil.

These insights can help us find a way forward in our
lives. While we can never escape the influence of the forces
which are expressed in the signs of the zodiac — for these
describe the structure of the world we live in — we are
able to develop our inherent potential in our own way. We
have complete power to use all the forces at our disposal
for good or evil. However, the responsibility for what

happens to the earth also lies in our hands. The forces of good await our acts with unconditional trust. It is only if we turn to them that they are able to work through us. If we do not, they must shift away from us and leave us to the forces of evil. These do not adopt a passive attitude, but impose themselves on us with all their power.

If we have a large share of the qualities of a particular sign of the zodiac and allow these qualities to develop separately without taking into account that they are part of a whole we would be turning towards the evil forces. It is even worse if we direct these qualities to areas in which they do not belong. It results in constant disharmony between our actions and the demands from around us.

This may cast light on one of Rudolf Steiner's central teachings: evil is essentially good, but is operating in the wrong area; evil is good which has been displaced.

Our powers and skills can therefore develop in a salutary way if we use them in the areas where they belong. If we do this not in a vague way but with detailed understanding, it is also possible to train these faculties and raise them to a high level. If we achieve a harmony between where we are and our own disposition, as in the case of animals, there is still a fundamental difference. For in us this achievement is entirely dependent on our own individual activities, while the animal has no choice.

But this does not answer the question of what we should do if we are faced with a task in a field which does not correspond with our nature? This is an important question, as most people are in the 'wrong place' in this sense. It is often necessary, particularly in a choice of profession, to restrain our disposition so that new skills can be acquired through practice. As everyone participates in all human activities, it could also be said that it will be necessary to develop weaker faculties while restraining stronger ones. The development of a person can also benefit if a particular disposition is restrained, leading to the appearance of more salutary aptitudes in another area.

In elaborating his ideas relating to the threefold division

of the social organism, Rudolf Steiner was particularly concerned with this question. He expected that in the field of the 'free spiritual life' there would be an area where everyone would be able to develop individual aptitudes as fully as possible. These may as yet be undeveloped in our work, but will later bear fruit for society.

Because we have control over our own capacities it is possible to raise these to a level far above normal. Thus the 'displacements' mentioned above which result from evil, may ultimately be for the good.

A knowledge of the relationship between the signs of the zodiac is one of the best foundations for understanding how to approach certain areas of life. In this way the signs of the zodiac can become a key to life, without which we come up against closed doors. With this knowledge at our disposal, we have freedom of movement, and can become kings in the realm of life. Rudolf Steiner pointed out that people who wish to act with total freedom not only have to grasp the ideas which they wish to pursue with their moral imagination, but also need a 'moral technique' to execute their ideas. By studying the laws of the zodiac we can gain important insights regarding this 'moral technique.'

Astrology teaches us that the life of every individual person is influenced to a large extent by the cosmic constellation at their birth. Therefore different signs of the zodiac and planets are predominant for every person. However, our lives are not simply an automatic process of characteristic themes determined by our own birth constellation. If we become aware that we have a destiny, the more we can feel called upon to find an area in which to determine this destiny. We can consciously learn to understand and use the unconscious, latent forces influencing us, while we float along the stream of life. Anyone who has mastered this field can deliberately introduce new themes into the current of destiny.

We shall now indicate in greater detail how the signs of the zodiac can become displaced if they are wrongly used, as well as how the signs can become our ideals to form our lives.

In describing the characteristic displacements or mistakes, we must take care to realize that it is only possible to take one example from an enormous spectrum.

In attempting to show how the signs can be held up as ideals, our task is even more difficult, for the individual creative forces should have free rein. So in mentioning a number of possible examples we hope that this will help others to find their own path. The signs of the zodiac, which are usually viewed as imperative images, can become liberating ideals. Thus they have been transformed from a strict rule book into a liberating manual.

Ideals are often despised because they are meaningless in real life. Often what are termed ideals are personal tendencies with little relation to the world — they are really illusions. However, those ideals which are rooted in a deeper world structure can develop great strength. All real progress is brought about by these true ideals.

The contribution we would like to make in this chapter is to provide a basis for a true idealism which is as exact and realistic as the most precise science. However, anything that stands in the way of achieving this should also be clearly described. It is only with this precise idealism that we will find the strength to lead the world towards good, and conquer evil.

Taurus and Scorpio

Scorpio is an image which has always been viewed as a special point of entry for the forces of evil. Obviously the Scorpio characteristics include some rather unpleasant aspects. For example, we saw how more than any other, the Scorpio character tends to break off the healthy relationship with the world as a whole. Obviously this does not apply in the same way for the animal, the scorpion, which, like any other animal, has its own special place in nature and is part of the whole. However, its whole lifestyle is such that it is an image of the condition of separation. It flees from the light which shines around it, and its form and movement expresses a bond with the earth which is not found in any of the other signs of the zodiac. This aspect is emphasized even more clearly in its relationship to the eagle, which seeks the light and escapes from the earth. A person who adopts the style expressed by this creature lives with the worst consequences of the fall from grace. Every detail indicates this. The creature's habit of paralysing its prey by raising it and separating it from its environment is expressed in the Scorpio character in the tendency to remove other creatures from their natural relationship with the world as a whole, so that they will serve him or her.

Evil forces are at work when man is torn away from his relationship with divine forces and puts his own interest first. In the worst Scorpio character this is adopted as an attitude to life. The Scorpio character's tendency to put their own desires first, and never to take into account the importance of other creatures or of their relationships, can be explained in these terms.

In an evil Scorpion character the evil can always be described as a sort of theft. Thieves also remove things from the place where they belong, to use to their own advantage. They will not make an effort themselves, but profit from other people's achievements. At a lesser level this can lead to sponging and swindling, but it can also result in merciless exploitation.

However, seemingly very different crimes can also be the result of Scorpio traits, such as betrayal, deceit, assassination, cruelty etc. These crimes are always carried out in a cold, calculating way in which the perpetrator's own desires are paramount and the victim's feelings count for nothing. In every case the path of least resistance is taken.

Scorpio tendencies can also lead to perversions of an erotic nature. When a man meets a woman a profound mutual deference can take place at every level. This meeting can lead to higher or exalted states, an openness for something to enter. The rigidity and separation of individuals are dissolved to make room for accessibility. Where Scorpio plays a role, every aspect of deference is opposed because the characters wish to determine everything themselves. This means that they are only able to take and cannot give in this field as well. Obviously this will lead to the urge to satisfy their desires at the expense of others.

Scorpio characters not only have the normal desires of every other creature, but also feel a particular wish for disharmony, to ruin other creatures and things, and even to make them suffer. When they feel like stealing something, it is not only to acquire it themselves but also to take it away from someone else. This even applies to their existence and happiness. (By contrast, Cancerians are satisfied and their own well-being enhanced when they merely add to their own possessions.

One of the positive tasks of the Scorpio character is to release us from the trudge of labour. In the past, slaves were used: in Ancient Greece for example people were oppressed, leading a purely physical existence, to enable others to live at a high cultural level. In our own time, this work should largely be performed by a more efficient organization of labour combined with extensive use of energy. To do this, labour and production methods must constantly be studied and ways found to achieve more with less effort. For the Scorpio, this is a matter of achieving the maximum effect with the minimum effort, by finding the right approach. It is already the case that we need to do so little work that we should have plenty of time and strength for our personal development.

However, by doing this, human beings have acquired tremendous forces which can be very easily misused. As long as we only use them to create a new and higher harmony, we are performing one of the highest tasks related to the development of the world. However, if these

forces are directed purely by our selfish will, we are sur-
rendering to the worst misuse of power.

We can see here how closely the highest good can border
on the worst evil, and can easily change into it.

Conversely, a questionable activity which the Scorpio
may engage in such as intrigue, can also be transformed
positively. In a community, communal life often fails to
develop properly because of all sorts of inhibitions. For
example, some people are withdrawn because of modesty
or anxiety and are unable to achieve many things for their
own benefit and for that of the community because of their
relationship with others. In this case, it can be very positive if a small remark or a little push, perhaps entirely or
wholly unnoticed, or even the careful passing on of something overheard in a personal conversation, leads to relationships being formed and exchanges taking place. Again
the Scorpio method can become a source of higher harmony. Instead of shortchanging or suppressing another
person, it can succeed in developing aspects which would
otherwise remain dormant. Thus the scorpion's venom is
used in a medicinal way!

In every type of activity involving a Scorpio character,
there is the separation of something from its context or its
liberation from all sorts of ties. The real purpose of this
sign lies in the liberation of all sorts of bonds imposed by
earthly existence, and the elevation to a higher harmony
which is in accordance with the world order.

The flight of an eagle is an image of this purpose.

While the Scorpio character tends to remove other creatures from their context, the Taurus character is in danger
of becoming too entrenched. This is expressed when the
creature charges towards an opponent and takes it onto his
horns. The head is no longer looking, but is all action.

Therefore things tend to go wrong when Taurus characters become leaders. They start becoming active themselves, plunging on without a clear understanding of the
situation, and without setting their helpers to work. If they

do set them to work, they will not achieve the right division of labour and the helpers may end up doing the same tasks that the leaders are doing. This results in an irritating waste of time and energy.

The Taurus character is particularly out of place in new situations for which there are no set rules or traditions. If they do come to face such a situation, this can lead to the disastrous sort of displacement referred to earlier.

However, when we surrender to our own Taurus forces, and allow them to take over, there are all sorts of dangers. For example, our actions can be determined too much by wild physical drives, or blind attacks of anger.

A very difficult situation may result when a Taurus character encounters a Scorpio character. For the latter it is tempting to take over the reins to see what can be done with so much strength and stupidity at their disposal (as they see it). They will be all the more successful because the Taurus creature is very easily taken over, and then his conduct tends to be determined from outside and he is ready to serve, as we discussed on page 88.

It often happens that people have gifts which they are unable to exploit to the full. For example, they may have unusual strength and stamina or extensive possessions, or an important position which gives them a great deal of influence. This may lead to a careless or unproductive use of their skills, or to a feeling of doubt, because life seems to have no content. Powers and skills which do not serve a good end become threatening, but they can be a blessing for the world when they unconditionally serve a higher task.

Wherever there is undirected power, something beneficial can be done for the community if the will to serve is developed. In fact, we all have a potential for this type of service. There are many tasks to be fulfilled which we can learn to see out of our own spiritual insights and which will promote the development of the world. As we never really know which task is confronting us we need to develop not only the potential for insights, but also the unconditional readiness to help bring about those things we consider necessary.

There is more to be learnt from the Taurus character. Repetitive and dull work must be performed in many areas of life, for example, small household tasks and simple jobs in the organizations of society. The people doing this work may experience a hopeless boredom. One soon feels that one is in the wrong place, and was intended for something better. This feeling can be so bad that one loses all sense of the purpose of life. It may help to realize that those routine daily tasks, like standing in ticket offices, working for the refuse disposal services, and many others, create a firm basis for the higher functions in society. These tasks are among the important things that need to be done. Ultimately these workers have a higher purpose. It is important that people who organize this kind of work constantly show their subordinates the real meaning of their work and its place in a larger context.

It is useful to know that the Taurus character always appeals for a purpose and guidance for his tremendous strength.

An example of the noblest Taurus character can be found in ancient tales in the life of Opherus, who became Christopherus. He was a tremendously strong, great hero, who set off to find the most powerful lord. For a time he served the devil, because he thought that was the greatest lord. However, he finally and unconditionally enters the service of Christ when he realizes that the devil fears Him.

We mentioned the aspects which can be learned from the eagle when we talked about positive intrigue. In fact, the eagle's soaring is based on a sort of intrigue. With the help of its sophisticated structure and careful attenuated movements, it senses sudden subtle changes in the airstream to gain height. In the same way there are possibilities in everyone's life for conquering the gravity and dulling forces of the earth by constant alertness, great presence of mind, and a tireless awareness that the purpose of life is ultimately linked to the development of the deeper essence of humankind.

Daily life, with its stream of unimportant events and the struggle for a secure existence, often demands more than seems reasonable. When our attention is drawn in too far, these problems seem to become even greater because, buried in the detail, we loose the overview. It can help to distance ourselves from the direct grind of daily life if every evening before going to sleep we pause and try to contemplate our situation in a wider context. Even in the most difficult situations it is possible to see oneself as though one were someone else. It is only possible to see the right relationships between things and their proper value from this bird's eye view. Something which previously looked like a mountain may turn out to be a molehill. Difficulties, which seemed unbearable at first, turn out to contain a wealth of possibilities for the future.

This also applies to humankind as a whole. There have always been great leaders, particularly during the darkest times, who were able to create images representing all development until far into the future. The best known example of this is the Revelation to St John. Those people who are capable of such insights have raised their visionary powers to such an extent that the laws of progressive development are opened up.

Rudolf Steiner's clear explanations and descriptions of the evolution of the world, and of humankind from the distant past to far in the future, can be a great help to people in our age. The language of images of an earlier age is made comprehensible to our thinking consciousness of today. These profound insights can help us soar above time on the wings of cosmic thoughts and develop an inner strength to face the weight of problems.

It is only by understanding these relationships that it is possible gradually to arrange life and raise it to such a level that it becomes an expression of profound spiritual background, with daily life being assimilated into the constant current of world events.

Leo and Aquarius

It is obvious that there are many areas in which the Leo character fully comes into its own. Great expertise based on a perfect knowledge of a particular subject, the strong management of a company in difficult circumstances, are examples of the Leo character.

However, again there may be a tendency to maintain this Leo attitude in inappropriate situations. Recognized experts may become so intolerant that they will not allow anyone to work with them. The head of an institute or a manager can inhibit the success of the organization because they will not tolerate independent colleagues. A strong desire to dominate can be the result of an inappropriate Leo attitude, and this type of Leo will claim a number of victims. Another example could be the mother of a young family. If she has a strong Leo character, this can result in dreadful tyranny.

However, we can also clearly see how someone who does not naturally have a Leo nature can be led by this sign. Anyone who has influence has attained a certain position. They must develop the strength to cope with every situation presented by life. They must learn to develop a relationship with the world as it is, even with the most pointless aspects. For example, if one wants to achieve anything in the scientific field, it is necessary to have a thorough understanding, even if the work up to that time has been one-sided and possibly confused. Managers in technical companies have to know everything that happens, know the workers, and have a knowledge of the product inside and outside the factory. They must be the centre where all these threads come together.

The Aquarius aspect is revealed particularly in helping other people. One should only really help when one can show other people the way to be more human and more themselves. However, it is all too common for people only to help or give things for their own satisfaction. This could be seen as a desire to serve or a desire to help, as opposed to a desire to dominate. What should only take place on the basis of the deepest insight can merely be the result of a drive, no better than any other drive, though it appears to be virtuous. This is a questionable aspect of some forms of philanthropy.

Another danger for the Aquarius character is that the sensitivity to a higher reality can lead to all sorts of dabbling in vague occultism, and a tendency to deal with hidden forces without understanding clearly what these are.

Some forms of unscientific healing, often interesting but tending towards charlatanism, are also closely related to Aquarian tendencies.

The highest demands are made by external circumstances on people who wish to achieve something in the world. It is easy to forget the true essence. One might even think that one's responsibility to the world was over when external duties are fulfilled and circumstances are under some control. However, it is important to continue to explore the meaning of being a person. This may be a waste of time in practical terms, but it has a salutary and ennobling effect on one's fellow human beings. The influence of imagery should never be underestimated. All people are profoundly influenced by the images from the environment affecting them. In turn, everyone is an environment for other people. Turning the world into a place where people can live in dignity is a great task. Everyone can help in this, merely by following a noble philosophy. Even if no one were to notice, our moral search is not in vain. We can feel confident that there are powers which safeguard the smallest aspects and assimilate them into the treasury of dignified humanity, acquired by humankind.

The search for inner development no longer means withdrawing from external life, as it used to in the past. However, one should strive to acquire, through concentration and meditation, an inner life in which one is entirely free of the strictures of the outer world. One should create an area where one is led only by spiritual desires and by higher human qualities. To achieve anything in the external world, one can use the strength of the Leo; to find a path in the inner world, one must be guided by a true image of man.

Although Aquarius represents a very high principle, Leo represents an image that is even higher. Christ at his greatest moment of glory is also represented as a lion. This is how it should be. When a divine creature descends into the sensory world, into the kingdom of the lion, and experiences all the resistance of solid matter while fully expressing their own essence, they are a lion in the highest sense. Just as the lion falls on its prey and tears it up, Christ opens up the material world in so far as it is dominated by anti-spiritual rigidity, and conquers it.

This brings us to the highest example which can serve as an ideal. In our inner development we must achieve a far-reaching conquest of our own nature, as well as a far-reaching transformation and control of our whole being, including our physical body. This also requires the strength and will of a lion, for it is only with these that we can conquer terrible resistance.

We are concerned here with the highest combination of Leo and man. In the natural world the lion devours other creatures, and sometimes even people. In man's world the strength of the lion only has any purpose if it clears the way for a truly divine principle.

Sagittarius and Gemini

A very dark problem is linked to the Sagittarian character. We will describe this as it appears when it is deeply rooted. It then bears similarities to Scorpio, although it is quite different. Both are all too aware of what they wish to achieve, and instinctively make use of everything to further their aims. But while Scorpio characters stand more or less outside the events for which they are responsible, people with the Sagittarian characters throw themselves into them. They are always engaged in a terrible struggle in which they jeopardize their own safety. Although it may be frightening to behold, the strength emanating from them is fascinating, and we can be drawn into it as into a thrilling spectacle.

We have already mentioned the separation of man from the divine tapestry of wisdom. The worst Scorpio character will use this for their own ends. They will creep in through the tear in this tapestry and take the broken threads into their own hands. By contrast, the Sagittarian character is more aware of the separation itself. While the Scorpion has little substance to sustain life, and therefore tends to be a parasite, Sagittarians have tremendous resources at their disposal and must learn to use them. This difference also determines the differences between the crimes that these two characters may perpetrate. If Scorpios are thieves, Sagittarians are more like robbers, taking what they want with violence. In this way, they are repeating the most basic problem of their nature. They experience the separation so strongly that they feel very far outside the divine order, and yet they have inherited a great deal of the divine substance. Therefore their nature is based on a sort of primeval robbery. They possess something which belongs in a larger context. They feel utterly lonely because they are totally alone in their separation. The only thing which is real to them is what they want themselves, their is own goals. Therefore they wish to clear out of the way everything that obstructs them, and will use any means to do so. In doing this, they do not enjoy the suffering of others, like the Scorpio character, but simply do not take their existence into account. Thus they are capable of murder if this corresponds with their goal. This could again be described as robbery, for they are robbing someone of their life. As they never act according to the customary order or norms, they will deceive and betray when they think this is necessary. However, they never do this for its own sake. They simply live in a world of their own norms and laws. This world is really only determined by the goal which inspires them. For them, the ends always justify the means.

It is clear that this type of separation will also lead to constant conflict with others.

Nowadays we are all too familiar with the raging of dark Sagittarian qualities. This was most clearly evident in National Socialism, which had some mad objectives leading to a tremendous concentrated development of strength. It lived on robbery, murder and deceit. It is clear that when one knows the background, even the spoken word was terribly misused to influence the will of the masses.* However, when we see how our whole age is virtually determined by the power struggle and conflict between economic powers and states, we become aware that we have all been concerned with the Sagittarian problem for a long time.

There are certain offences against the deeper world order which are particularly noticeable, so that society can defend itself against them through the power of the law, but there are others which are hardly noticed. And yet these offences are hardly any less serious than the criminal ones.

The study of the zodiac can reveal this. Every character is in danger of committing certain offences against the world order. However, how many people are there who understand that the 'desire to help' can be a negative tendency? (See page 153)

Obviously the weaknesses of the Gemini character will not easily cause conflict with the law. They intervene too little in events. And yet if an ethereal Gemini character has a position of responsibility, they may merely try to enjoy life and will fail to notice problems. The matters under their control may become hopelessly confused, and

---

* Karl Heyer gave a perfect description of this characteristic in his book *Wenn die Götter den Tempel verlassen* [When the Gods leave the temple] Novalis, Freiburg 1947.

this can lead to terrible disaster. They may not be the actual instigator, but it is the result of their frivolity. A doubting nature can lead to the same problems.

Now that we have indicated some problems related to Sagittarius and Gemini, it is clear how these two images can be used as important keys for approaching the right areas.

Many people have a strong will and yet achieve little in life. This is often because their attention is fragmented. They become involved in one thing and then another, and there is no fixed course to direct their lives. Sagittarians always have a specific target. They carefully consider what they want to achieve, and even when to achieve it. Why not have goals which can only be reached in many years' time? When they set their goal, they take the firm decision to pursue it at all costs. Obviously life makes other demands. They may not be afraid to make detours, but nevertheless they always keep their goal in mind and unswervingly moves towards its realization. This attitude has a magical effect. It is as though they have recruited the powers of heaven and earth. When the secret of the goal is known, one can take on tasks which seem impossible. They are like hunters pursuing a quarry; they are able to penetrate areas which would have inspired them with fear in any other situation.

We can appreciate how the whole world is full of wonderful wisdom and beauty. Our everyday surroundings, and even the simplest things, are connected to the greatest power. If we constantly set ourselves difficult goals and try to impose our will, we might blindly rush past the greatest wealth. Gemini, childlike characters, can teach us to discover the miracle in everything. For this we have to look around us attentively, and always be prepared to surrender completely to the simplest phenomena. We must learn to displace ourselves into other areas, and develop an empathy with all things. Then our whole environment will flourish and reveal wonders which we didn't even dare to dream about. True interest is like a magic lantern, and its glow makes many secrets shine. In this way we can discover that everything, no matter how seemingly insignificant, still contains an element of value.

However, there are more serious tasks which are represented by Gemini. Dark destructive forces are raging with increasing violence everywhere in the world. Crime is growing at such a rate that it sometimes seems as though there will soon be no place at all for the noble will. Even the most severe punishments no longer help. For how can someone be restrained from deviating behaviour if there is no possibility for them to learn to take the right path? In our present culture we are suffering from a predominant focus on materialism and technology. Therefore the human soul is chained to heavy and physical elements, and is separated too much from the realms of light where it originated. If evil is combatted in the same violent way by destroying all its offshoots, it will only become stronger than ever. In the moral field it is not possible to use force to destroy force. There is a law of conservation of energy. If the power of evil has been suppressed in one field, it will develop all the more strongly in another. It is a power which must be conquered by being transformed and used for building. Nature can teach us how to do this: Plants counter the power of gravity in completely aiming at expanding and growing upwards. They gain strength to do this from the most delicate and noble of all natural forces, from light.

In the moral field, it is only possible to achieve something against the forces of darkness by a positive and confident attitude. This great force should be recruited and evil effects should be converted into good. It should never be forgotten that, even in the foundations of the worst evil, there is a profound desire to be reunited with the highest divine element from which everything was created. Only those who find access to the depths where that desire lives can truly transform this into goodness. Only the purest forces, especially those of the child, have access to these depths. When adults arouse the childlike element within them, and their maturity is led by this, they will be able to conquer evil. Now, as never before, there seems to be a tendency to destroy this childlike element, and yet the future lies in the hands of the child. Only the child in man can illuminate the darkness and lead us towards a radiant future.

On attaining profound insights from anthroposophy there is always a danger that one will be content to enjoy the radiant light emanating from acquired knowledge. However, sympathy must be aroused for the terrible suffering that is experienced all over the earth. This can lead to a resolve not to rest until one's philosophy has developed into a completely new cultural life. There is no activity in any field, whether technology, agriculture, education or art, which should not be approached with the help of spiritual guidelines on a new basis. The Sagittarian can teach us to develop such forces, so that, surrounded by the old culture, one will have the courage to establish institutions and carry out new activities which are entirely directed by the light emanating from true spiritual science. In the middle of an old and decaying culture it will be possible to create a new and flourishing world.

Virgo and Pisces

For the Virgo character there is always a danger that she will become so secluded and rigid that the development of germination will be inhibited rather than stimulated.

For instance, a household requires care and order which can be a benefit to children. However, if order and tidiness become important for their own sake, the children can hardly move and their development is stunted.

There are people who are not in the least interested whether the world around them is sinking into chaos and despair, as long as their own affairs are neatly ordered. This could apply to people who have a beautifully furnished and carefully maintained large house just for themselves. Others may have a valuable collection which they do not share with anyone. In these cases it is not so much a matter of the monetary value of these things, which would be the case for the Cancerian character, but the things themselves and their special quality. The *Lady of Stavoren* story describes this problem.

The same story also describes another problem. At the beginning of the story the Lady of Stavoren is told that the most valuable thing is missing from her table. When she sends her captains out and the last one returns with grain, claiming it to be the most valuable thing, he is fulfilling his mission, for she had no bread on her table. However, she has the grain thrown overboard with the result that the town is impoverished, and she later starves to death. What had she done for fate to be so harsh with her? The imagery of bread or grain usually refers to the body of Him who broke the bread and said: 'Take ye and eat, for this is my body.' She is rejecting the body of the resurrected Lord which can restore life, and she only seeks external splendour, the world of gold.

This is such a grave offence that it has a catastrophic effect on the course of history, although it has hardly been recognized as such. In a true culture, cooperation with spiritual realities is essential. These are so elevated, and often so difficult to understand for daily consciousness, that the meaning can only be borne and received if one adopts the same restrained and pure attitude as the Virgin adopts towards her child.

The meaning of the central Christian image, the Last Supper, consists in passing the resurrection to the participating community. What has happened in the past? On the one hand, the power to maintain this image has been endlessly misused, while on the other hand, there is increasing confusion about its significance. The greatest mercy shown to man on earth is increasingly accepted in an impure way, and even rejected altogether. For a long time man has suffered spiritual hunger in the deepest sense. Around us we see how man is also suffering great physical starvation. This is the harsh reality of the predictions in the story of *The Lady of Stavoren*. The story tells us that rejecting the body of the resurrected Lord is the ultimate cause of physical starvation.

A virgin's betrayal of grain is also a theme in *Ein Kampf um Rom* when Mataswintha sets fire to the granaries during the great siege of Ravenna. Again this results in a dreadful disaster.

In the Pisces character there is always a danger of a lack of restraint. For instance, this may give rise to companionable drinking carousing and revelry. Everyone buys rounds of drinks, and everyone must have a share, and everybody must have as much fun as everybody else. However, when people with the Pisces character do not have enough themselves, they are equally happy to make free with other people's possessions, and this tendency can develop into straightforward swindling. In this character the distinction between yours and mine becomes vague both directions.

In the real Pisces character there is a constant flow. They are unable to hold onto anything, so that possessions are always streaming in and out. This tendency may be ideal for trade and commerce where this constant movement also takes place. Things that belong to one person one moment belong to another the next. In many cases it is even necessary to deal entirely with other people's possessions.

This aspect of exchange and the transfer of goods, which takes place among humans in the form of trade, can also be found between different species of animals. Only there the transfer takes place in the form of one animal eating another, something which fish exemplify to a very high degree.

The interaction related to trade also leads to the cross-fertilization of nations. It is evident that trade depends upon the exchange of goods, and if it is carried out properly, each party benefits.

Having either too much or too little of something is unsatisfactory. One of the virtues of the Pisces character is a sensitivity to this, so that they can improve the situation by interacting with others. It is almost self-evident that the great impetus for the transition from the Middle Ages to our own age, the Piscean era, came from a number of seafaring nations. Portugal, Holland and England took the lead in rapid succession. The age of Pisces is characterized by voyages of searching and discovery throughout the world. Trade and commerce have led to an interaction between all nations. This has had an enriching effect, especially for those nations which took the initiative. On the other hand, much suffering has been caused. Whole nations have been wiped out, enslaved, died out or degenerated. This reveals an aspect of the great defect which can be related to the Pisces character. Because of the tremendous tendency to expand, there is a threat that we become completely externalized. This means that we lose the inner bond with our origin and become evil, bringing death and decay. Just as the threat in the Virgo character lies in her rejection of what she should receive, Pisceans may merely take while they should give and take. When this happens, they bring only death and decay.

How can we make we make the most of the good qualities of the Virgo character?

The story of *The Lady of Stavoren* warns us that it is bad to look too much at the external aspects of the world. This could result in hunger and misery. What can we do to avert this disaster? Instead of looking at the external world, we can concentrate on the internal world. Valuable seeds of life are dormant not only in the human soul, but also in the realm of nature. Observing these reveals an element which can have a profound and beneficial effect on cultural life when it is assimilated and allowed to flourish. However, to achieve this it is necessary to approach these phenomena with virginal spirituality. At every moment nature is prepared to provide us with the highest things, but normally we crudely reject it. For example, scientific phenomena are usually only taken seriously if they fit the predetermined aims. The colours of flowers are used for classification; chemical reactions are observed only to prove or disprove a particular theory. However, it is possible to approach these phenomena for their own sake.* If we take them in with an open mind and allow them space in our imagination, they will blossom of their own accord and reveal their real content.

As a scientist Goethe was a master of this phenomenological method. Anyone who follows this method finds that things are revealed which are of enormous importance for the healthy development of society.

The sign of Pisces shows us where there may be fertile soil with little growth because the right seed has not been sown. The soul of a child is often like such soil. If children are given too many abstract concepts, they are unable to develop this in the wonderful and delicate inner life that is constantly unfolding. Everything assimilated by children should be full of life and germinating force, like the seed of a plant. Such a germinating force can be found, for instance, in the images of fairy-tales. These are joyfully received; for a long time they appear to be dormant while they combine with deeper developmental processes. Many years later they can mature into inner richness and security, and have a beneficial effect in the world. A true fairy-tale can never be fully understood. It contains a secret, a miracle like every living creature, and it is this miracle which makes it so effective.

This brings us to one of our most important points. Our

---

* Henry David Thoreau expressed this scientific dilemma beautifully: 'I, standing twenty miles off, see a crimson cloud on the horizon. You tell me it is a mass of vapour which absorbs all other rays and reflects the red, but that is nothing to the purpose ... What sort of science is that which enriches the understanding, but robs the imagination? If we knew all things thus mechanically merely, should we know anything really?'

culture is increasingly dominated by intellectual and abstract thought, and the question is rarely asked what effect this type of thought has on the human spirit. The effect is the opposite of that of a fairy-tale; it kills something in the soul and detracts from the life force. To a large extent the inability to recreate our human society is the result of these deadening thought processes. In order to discover the creative forces which build up our culture, it is necessary for the thought processes to penetrate the realms of life. In his *Metamorphosis of Plants*, Goethe sowed the seed of a science which makes this possible. Nowadays, anyone can pursue this goal on the basis of a training in spiritual science. It is strange that it is first necessary to arouse the thinking processes, and combine the life forces with these processes, before it is possible to gain an understanding of the areas of life. However, this type of thinking also has a stimulating and fruitful effect on others.

Studying the works of Rudolf Steiner, we find that his thoughts are full of this life-giving effect. Even his apparently crisp and cool ideas contain a wealth of hidden potential developments. In this type of thought there is no distinction between science and art.

Training our thought processes to think in images is a way of developing this skill. When we are able to think in images in accordance with the profound laws of the world, we learn to use and form our own life forces.

Capricorn and Cancer

In the sign of Capricorn, as with Sagittarius and Scorpio, there are indications of a special link with evil. Again the problem of separation is clearly apparent.

While the Sagittarian character often experiences its separation from the world as a tragedy, and the Scorpio character is all too inclined to separate other creatures from their natural context, people of the Capricorn character tend proudly to raise themselves above others. The tradition of Lucifer's revolt and rebellion against heaven is reminiscent of the Capricorn attitude. The devil is often depicted with cloven hooves and other goat-like attributes.

At a very primitive level, the instinct to ignore everything and determine everything in a selfish way is no more than an eccentric tendency. The desire to oppose the world can merely be a way of attracting attention. When it goes further, it can lead to a life of wandering and adventure. In general there is a tendency to act on every whim. The Capricorn character may be called capricious.

Even the love of heights, if overdeveloped, can lead to terrible arrogance and a contempt for others.

The Capricorn character contains the urge to venture everything and go to extremes. These characteristics can take man to the highest achievements, for there are areas where there is absolutely no help or support available from outside, and which can only be attained independently in great loneliness. We enter these domains when we wish to gain an insight into the secret depths of the world. We can only go as far as we can take ourselves. Even when the insight that is sought is discovered in clear terms, it is still like a sheer cliff to be scaled with our own strength. At best, other people can indicate the direction to take, but, essentially, a tremendous personal effort is needed to progress further.

There are two characteristics which play an important part in this respect: courage and independence. But these characteristics can also lead one into contact with evil.

The figure of Faust is undoubtedly driven by his love of heights. His courage is unshakable and he is free of all prejudice. He wishes to transcend every border and every tradition, and will not be conquered by any power in the world. When he no longer succeeds in attaining the spiritual heights which were once accessible to the best men, he starts to use magic to invoke spirits. He tries to attract the powers which he can no longer reach in their own sphere. In this way he is increasingly led along the path of evil. Therefore his search for the highest things leads him into terrible depths. When we study the dramatic content of this destiny, we are confronted with the tragedy of modern man. Science is based on the desire to conquer prejudice, to break through restrictive traditions. Every true scientist prefers to jeopardise their soul rather than give up their independent search. However, while the valuable jewel of independence is achieved in this way, the lowest forces of the world are revealed and exploited to an increasing extent. All around us, we see powers in technology which are no longer under the control of those who summoned them up. It is precisely these forces which are increasingly employed for the purposes of destruction, allowing evil to have an extremely destructive effect on our times.

The inclination to ignore boundaries can also lead to extraordinary excesses in the erotic field. This is expressed in stories of witches, when a witch anoints herself from top to toe with her potions to change her consciousness in such a way that she feels she is floating off and experiencing great adventures. This example of decadent initiation ceremonies represents a spiritual search and the liberation of physical concerns, but as it is achieved by inappropriate methods, the witch enters a dubious realm. A noteworthy description of this can be found in Goethe's *Faust*, as well as in *Leonardo* by Merejkovski, where there is a strange combination of erotic sensations with the appearance of a superhuman goat figure.

The problems of the Cancer character have already been described in detail. These involve not so much wild or base crimes as weaknesses or shortcomings which can also have dubious results. The lack of courage, the small-mindedness, the morbid caution, blindness to everything which transcends the basest things are obvious negative traits. In worse cases, there may be terrible avarice which in turn can lead to the exploitation of other people. However, there is another Cancerian tendency which has just as bad an influence as the familiar problems mentioned above, though it is not clear whether it should be considered as an offence or a sickness. This is the elaboration and dissemination of a materialist philosophy. This may have turned man's attention to external phenomena, resulting in tremendous cultural achievements, as well as the progression of human thinking in terms of independence, clarity and solidity. Yet materialism turns away from the divine origin of things so that evil forces, unnoticed, gain an ever-stronger hold on human activities. It denies the existence of any spiritual power and therefore promotes the effect of those spirits which wish to influence us unconsciously, while opposing the effect of the forces of good which help us to grow into fully conscious creators and co-workers.

The Cancer sign can also be an ideal, just like the Capricorn. This is the sign which constantly reminds us of our responsibility. People on their own can follow individual whims and caprices without being punished, and a lifestyle full of change and adventure will not hurt them. However, caring for a family or looking after any other sort of community involves responsibilities. One does one's best to do all the daily tasks in a regular and orderly fashion. Foresight is needed and plans made to ensure survival. For example, one must have a regular income, and ensure against changing circumstances. If there is no base like this for daily life, all one's energy will be sapped by continual worry. But if there is ground under one's feet and a roof over one's head, then the social and spiritual life of the community can flourish.

However, no matter how solid this base is, situations can still arise in which the ground seems to disappear under one's feet, for instance, when one is overcome by an accident. One has to summon the Capricorn element, for everything now relies totally on one's own courage and presence of mind. Every action is a struggle, and everything depends on the rapid development of great spiritual strength. Those who can feel proud in their independence and can mock the circumstances thwarting them, are fortunate. If the Cancerian element remains predominant, all will be lost.

Even in the area of inner life, problems may arise which can only be solved with the meticulous care of a Cancer character. People who wish to develop their inner life so that they are able to acquire the highest spiritual insights, must transform their lives by turning away from physical considerations and towards spiritual aspects. There is a danger of becoming alienated from external life because the interest is turned towards other areas. One might have great powers and yet come to grief because of a careless approach to everyday life. To prevent this, it is necessary patiently to train the thoughts, feelings and the will step-by-step. The spiritual forces which interact with external life need to be strengthened before one can turn inwards. In this way it is possible to build a base in external life which will give support in all circumstances and for all inner experiences.

Aries and Libra

Typical Aries characters tend to view their own ideas as being so real that they will pursue them in the face of any external opposition. If the ideas are good and beneficial, it may be positive to develop a love of conflict. In this case, Aries characters are where they belong.

However, this love of conflict all too easily turns into fanaticism. Fanatical Aries characters only take into account their own ideas, or even a single idea, and try to gain recognition for it, pursuing it at all costs. In this respect their strength can be very destructive and they can even become troublemakers who are not concerned so much with a particular idea as with being proved right for its own sake.

Historically, the rigid Aries character has led to serious misdeeds, particularly during religious conflicts. Again and again doctrines have been turned into dogma which has been imposed upon others. Those who refused to accept this were mercilessly persecuted.

People of the Libra character tend to assign greater weight to the insights and the will of other people than to their own. This attitude can be appropriate as long as the ideas and the people concerned are valuable and can lead to something good. However, there have also been circumstances in history in which a strong character and a capacity for making sharp distinctions has been necessary.

True Libras certainly wish to achieve something which they can do on their own, although they may follow other people a long way. This can become problematical if it is taken to extremes, with people deciding that it is always easiest to follow the most powerful influence around.

Every organization relies on co-operation and develops certain forms of procedures for reaching decisions. This may result in things getting into a rut. For example, a factory using an old method when there are new technical possibilities faces these problems. It is important to acquire the best and latest insights and use these to change the company or organization. A great deal of courage and perseverance is needed to introduce these because the existing balance must be broken to achieve a new order. If the changes are not entirely successful, there is a danger that more is destroyed than improved. This is the lesson which Aries teaches us.

On a higher level we are faced with a similar problem. If we are inspired by spiritual ideals which penetrate life like a beacon shining in the future, we find the surrounding culture which is to be transformed by these ideals is resistant to change, and even to a recognition of the spirit. From the spiritual point of view there is great darkness and turgidity in cultural life. It is one of the highest tasks of the Aries character to introduce spiritual ideas to the world with strength and courage. Only when they succeed can humankind continue to develop.

The Libra character teaches us very different, but equally important matters.

One may be in a situation where one has to work together with different people who have creative gifts and persevere by force of their own will. This can lead to disharmony because everyone would collide, and a great deal of strength would be lost, in pushing aside each other's achievements. One can achieve a positive effect by restraining one's own will and allowing the strength of other people to create a harmony and interaction. Even someone with very little strength can have a beneficial influence by acting as an intermediary in a tactful way. Where there is rhythm and balance, the forces of good with some rational strength can combine with events.

Anyone who begins an inner development is immediately faced with the demand to take everything that is happening within them just as seriously as events in the outside world. One is striving to reach inwardly the creative powers whose creation is the visible world. Here one penetrates a realm that has greater reality than the experiences of daily life. This may endanger one's normal relationship with the world and with other people, though this should not happen in healthy development. One has to live two lives which are inherently opposed to one another. If one obeys unconditionally the demands of one of these worlds, one will be distracted away from the direction of the other. Human beings can only achieve the highest levels when their eyes are open to the demands of the outside world, and are still able to fulfil the task set by their inner lives.

7. The Sun's Annual Path and Human Character

To conclude this work it is necessary to show how the sun/earth constellation is expressed in the twelve characters. So far we have related the sun's annual path to the lives of the creatures of the zodiac, and these creatures to human characteristics. But we have not explored the direct reflection of the sun's path in the human character. To avoid a lengthy repetition, we will give a few indications to serve as a key and leave the rest to the reader.

In the time of Gemini the sun is high in the heaven and still continues to rise. The earth reflects its abundance of light in the wealth of flowers, the play of insects and innumerable other creatures. The true Gemini character's relation to his environment is like that of the sun to the earth at this time: they spread radiance and splendour everywhere. This is because of the loose connection of their higher self with the body.

During the time of Cancer the sun ceases this upward movement and starts to pull towards the earth. The trees start to form buds and store reserves of nutrients in the trunk, looking after future needs in general. In the same way the Cancerian character is particularly concerned with the material side of existence. Their higher self is only permitted to play a minor role. Their life is almost entirely determined by circumstance, that is, not by matters which arise from their inner nature.

In thus relating the cosmic constellation to the corresponding phenomena in the life of human beings, another important relationship is revealed between the different characters. Following the sun's movements through the zodiac every year, and comparing the corresponding human characters, each successive sign always seems to contain a correction for the one-sidedness and shortcomings of the previous sign. This illustrates the strict balance in the structure of the cosmos. Every movement of the sun at a certain time of year appears to be placed on a pair of scales and the contrary movement takes place at another time of the year.

These contrasts are also found between people and groups of people, but there is nothing to force them to accept a balance with their counterpart. While the sun always continues in its orbit, it is all too easy for human beings to lose their way and develop in one-sided ways.

If this balance did not exist, the sun would become completely alienated from the earth during the time of Gemini. It is this tendency to lose the relationship with the reality of earthly life that is a particular threat to the Gemini character.

In contrast, the Cancerian character is concerned primarily with real life. If the sun followed only the direction which it has in the time of Cancer, it would betray its true light nature for ever and be completely captured by earthly forces. Thus Cancerian characters are always in danger of losing themselves in their fear of circumstances.

The Leo character's own nature is always powerfully predominant and they feel the need to be in control of circumstances.

In this way we can distinguish even more clearly the importance of small changes and movements in the constellation. The movement of the sun never has a constant quality, it is always in transition and gradually changing. By projecting this onto earthly life, we see that these changes are also part of the great cosmic balance. Examining this fluid movement in great detail reveals a one-sidedness in every fragment of the sun's orbit which is immediately defeated. This takes us another step further into the elevated cosmic order.

8. The Cosmic Order and the Social Order

As the life of animals is completely determined by an all-encompassing wisdom of which they are unconscious, the interrelationship between animals is also part of a single great order.

For man this is no longer the case, and in the course of history this link has constantly diminished. There is still an order, but it is largely man-made. It is based on a tradition which is only partly instinctive, but is largely derived from the religious manifestations revealed to great leaders.

We now face the problem that the substance of tradition is virtually used up, while the residual healthy instincts retained by man have an increasingly questionable character. This is inevitable, as all human activities must increasingly be led by independent thought. However, this thought, as it has developed up to now, does not provide any guidelines for a healthy society. It is trained by dead nature and it is concerned with problems related to the laws of life.

If no new guidelines are provided with sufficient strength, human development has reached a stage of bankruptcy.

How can we discover these new guidelines? The path shown by Rudolf Steiner is as follows: 'You must independently penetrate those spheres which also feed the springs which watered earlier civilizations.' He gave many instructions of how this could be done.

But this is not enough. In fact, it is demanding rather too much. Many people will not be able to follow this difficult path straightaway. And yet everyone should have an opportunity to acquire the necessary insights. The time in which the masses were semi-consciously or unconsciously led is past.

Rudolf Steiner also complied with this demand. He made so much information available from the spring which he mentions, that anyone can discover and understand the guidelines for living in society, if they make an effort.

Above all, Steiner referred to nature as a great teacher, saying 'We will not gain any social impulses in any way except by assimilating spiritual insights from nature all around us.'

This point of view was the main guideline for this book. We have derived deeper insights regarding the human character from nature around us and can transform these into guidelines to build up a new society.

This sheds some light on some of the most urgent problems facing society.

What is the purpose of the endless conflicts which dominate our lives? We have learned to see that conflict is a basic principle. Every polarity between two contrasting images is a fundamental image of some contrast between people or between situations. When we understand this, and then focus our attention on the signs of the zodiac, it provides us with the challenge to overcome the contrasts derived from the past. Once our thoughts contained this question, and now it is like a deep call to the will.

We are able to become free and creative beings because of the fact that the world is full of imperfections, and because of the conflicts from which we suffer. They form the field which we can tackle independently. In the introduction we mentioned that the lives of animals *unconsciously* answer questions which they do not understand. At a much higher level this is a guideline for our own lives. Our lives could be a *conscious* answer to questions which were left unanswered by the divine forces during creation, and which we can clearly understand.

Another problem in life is the painful experience that people with greater powers than others often have weaknesses which the average person simply considers ridiculous. This phenomenon is also easy to understand. It is one of the basic principles of the world order that every power leads to some shortcoming. This applies to man just as it does to the animals. Understanding this, we can accept one-sidedness in others: however, it leads to the greatest intolerance when we become aware of our own one-sidedness. For this basic principle is part of the natural world order which independent creative man must transform into a new order. Being human means having an instinct to rise above the natural order. Again this poses a question of life, but this time it is posed by our own past.

It is not only the contrasts and conflicts which give rise to questions, but also the wealth of human qualities which we encounter in life and which can become an enormous problem. This can lead us to the depths of despair and an inconsolable feeling of worthlessness, for we hardly seem to have access to the greatest aspect of human qualities.

In contrast, at the right moment we should base our self-awareness on what we are. Each of us has qualities which are superior to those of others. If we have the courage to accept that we only represent a fragment of the full range of human qualities, this painful insight can be transformed into one of the strongest creative forces. In particular, it provides a basis for building a better society. Only this enables each of us to take up a particular place with all our strength, at the same time leaving space for others. Usually we fight to be at the front, but we would get much further if we used the same force to fight for other people's places. If we learn to understand how a particular person's disposition suits particular areas of life and particular tasks, we can also learn to follow a path and ask the questions which allow new growth.

This is one of the most important points which can be used in a concrete way to fight against evil.

We discussed how evil arises when there are displacements in the world order, that is, when forces operate at a time or in a place where they do not belong. When we are aware of this, it is often possible to prevent disastrous events by making minor adjustments, for example, directing forces, which are having the wrong effect in one field, to another field where they have a positive effect.

However, there are many more far-reaching possibilities if we do not merely direct these forces to good effect in particular cases, but raise ourselves up to one of the greatest ideals which can be espoused in our existence on earth: living in an order which can reflect the order of the stars. This enables us to become bearers of cosmic forces and have a profound creative and transforming effect in life on earth.

There was a time when this ideal was practised. There were twelve in Christ's company. These matters seem very distant, but perhaps the reason our society is so chaotic is because the order of the stars is unable to reign and there are few people who consciously know or want this.

It is rarely necessary for the actual number twelve to be there in the outside world, but if our lives are based on the insights of the wisdom in the stars, the twelvefold order can have a powerful creative effect. Perhaps it rarely happens that there is no one to fulfill a certain place. In this case, another person must fulfill that task. An ideal community will require these sacrifices. One person may simply fulfill their own tasks fully and retreat from places where others should develop. The task of another may be to allow a friend to go his or her own way, though this may seem very strange. For yet another, it is the fulfilment of a task which does not really suit them. A true community is only achieved when all the participants devote themselves unconditionally to their own tasks, lighting their own flames so that altogether they burn together as a tremendous fire.

In this fire the flames of the spirit will be able to come down and arouse the storms of enthusiasm, giving us the strength and courage to transform our dark earth into a true society for humankind.